Titles published in English by the Academic Network

G. Corbae · J. B. Jensen · D. Schneider
Marketing 2.0
VI, 151 pages. 2003. ISBN 3-540-00285-5

S. Dutta · A. De Meyer · A. Jain
G. Richter (Eds.)
The Information Society
in an Enlarged Europe
X, 290 pages. 2006. ISBN 3-540-26221-0

Michael Blatz
Karl-J. Kraus
Sascha Haghani

Editors

Corporate Restructuring

Finance in Times of Crisis

With 64 Figures
and 2 Tables

 Springer

Strategy Consultants

Michael Blatz
Karl-J. Kraus

Roland Berger
Strategy Consultants GmbH
Alt Moabit 101b
10559 Berlin, Germany
E-mail: michael_blatz@de.rolandberger.com
E-mail: karl-j-kraus@de.rolandberger.com

Dr. Sascha Haghani

Roland Berger
Strategy Consultants GmbH
Karl-Arnold-Platz 1
40474 Düsseldorf, Germany
E-mail: sascha_haghani@de.rolandberger.com

Cataloging-in-Publication Data
Library of Congress Control Number: 2006922371

ISBN-10 3-540-33074-7   Springer Berlin Heidelberg New York
ISBN-13 978-3-540-33074-5   Springer Berlin Heidelberg New York

Springer is a part of Springer Science+Business Media
springeronline.com

© Springer-Verlag Berlin Heidelberg 2006
Printed in Germany

Cover design: Erich Kirchner
Production: Helmut Petri
Printing: Strauss Offsetdruck

SPIN 11692232   Printed on acid-free paper – 42/3153 – 5 4 3 2 1 0

Foreword

Technological progress and globalization have completely changed the overall conditions and rules of entrepreneurial engagement. The speed of this modern high performance economy has accelerated, competition is fiercer than ever, and the battles are no longer fought in the domestic or intra-European arena, but on a global level. To keep up with their rivals and increase their productivity, businesses must be able to efficiently manage their processes and structures. However, strategies and business models must be developed simultaneously to set the stage for a successful and sustainable course of expansion.

Driven by these forces, the management and focus of restructuring measures has also changed in recent years: in the past, the primary objective was to implement solutions to improve the operational end of the business – and, ultimately, to cut costs. The strategic revamping of the company is closely linked to this type of operational restructuring. Since then, however, another financial dimension has been added to this restructuring approach. In other words, the restructuring process – and the respective demands it imposes on stakeholders, such as managers, financial partners, and consultants – has evolved substantially from pure cost cutting measures (often associated with "rightsizing") to consulting on the brink of insolvency (planned insolvency method) and growth-oriented financial restructuring.

In the recent past numerous companies have been forced to implement comprehensive restructuring programs. They met the challenge head-on and were thus in a position to improve their cost situation, as well as the management of their structures and processes. Nevertheless, after they had done their operational homework, many businesses discovered that they were caught in a growth trap: cost adjustment is one of the essential prerequisites for corporate success, but on its own it does not suffice. To be successful in the long term, companies must increase their revenues through new strategic approaches, and thus embark on a path of profitable growth. Success hinges on the implementation of a parallel restructuring and growth strategy. Our latest surveys show that the stock market value of a company more than doubles if its strategy focuses on costs and growth simultaneously.

In less supported markets the understanding that there is a much greater need overall for strategic challenges as well as strategies for more growth and permanent operational optimization prevailed much sooner than was the case in this country. Consequently, concentration on growth is much more pronounced in other European countries than it is in Germany. Most German businesses lack the financial resources for implementation of expansive corporate strategies. This is primarily the result of the fact that in Germany – unlike the situation in other

European countries – "classic" forms of business funding, such as bank loans, still dominate the scene; although a whole range of alternative financing instruments, which have long penetrated the Anglo-American business world, is available. Among the options are private equity funding or so-called mezzanine financing, a product filling the niche between equity financing and shareholder capital (for example jouissance rights and bonds). To date, these financing types still play a subordinate role in Germany. In particular, medium-sized companies are reluctant to take advantage of these options and tend to prefer the more traditional bank loans, although there is a lot of evidence that companies that rely on a combination of various methods of financing are more successful. Moreover, the credit policies of banks have changed significantly; given their own profit-strapped environment and the more stringent equity capital requirements imposed by Basel II, most financial institutions are also unwilling to increase their credit liabilities and are pursuing restrictive risk-averting policies.

Under these circumstances, companies would do well to rethink their existing growth funding strategies: financial restructuring through recapitalization is available as a potential solution, as it represents an improvement in the liabilities scenario. Private equity funding can be used as an alternative or in combination with recapitalization. During and after restructuring measures, the rearrangement of corporate financing is particularly complex. Mastering this task hinges on precise know-how and the ability to handle all corporate finance tools. Consequently the Restructuring & Corporate Finance Competence Center has compiled this book to provide an overview of the key aspects that should be taken into consideration during financial restructuring. The content is based on experience and knowledge gained in more than 1,700 restructuring projects performed since 1980.

Another objective of the book is to highlight the changed restructuring success factors. To achieve this, we provide reports of our experiences in numerous restructuring projects and summarize the latest studies we have performed and published in this regard. We also place great emphasis on a practical focus; based on anonymous case studies we describe how the new approaches to corporate financing can be applied concretely. This book is an extension of our previous publications on restructuring, and in terms of content should be understood as a continuation.[1] The reports target experienced professionals who want to obtain an overview of the current developments in terms of corporate recapitalization.

---

[1] For example "Restrukturierung, Sanierung und Insolvenz" (Restructuring, Reorganization and Insolvency) by Buth, Andrea/Hermanns, Michael (Editors) 1998, "Die Unternehmenskrise als Chance" (Corporate Crisis as an Opportunity) by Bickhoff, Nils/Blatz, Michael/Eilenberger, Guido/Haghani, Sascha/Kraus, Karl-J. (Editors) 2004.

To meet this objective, the book has been divided into three parts:

– *Part 1* comprises five articles, which look at the progression and success factors of restructuring processes in Germany from various perspectives: the introductory article summarizes the corporate crisis management concepts in a status quo report and shows what direction these approaches will have to take in the future. The second article evaluates restructuring under the general economic conditions in Germany and works out the recipe for restructuring success. In the third article, the author provides an insight into the current status of the discussion on financial restructuring and introduces the recapitalization concept. The forth article presents the financial action options open to medium-sized companies, the content of a restructuring concept, as well as strategies for negotiations with financial partners. The final article emphasizes the changes in due diligence requirements from the perspective of potential financial investors. Due to the fact that traditional criteria for risk assessment focus primarily on the past and on the status quo, this article makes a case for altering the assessment criteria for restructuring companies.

– *Part 2* reinforces the importance of financial restructuring based on the results of the latest surveys performed by Roland Berger Strategy Consultants. The Roland Berger European restructuring survey evaluates success factors and restructuring trends in Western, Central, and Eastern Europe. The study is based on interviews with approximately 2,600 executives, which were carried out in the second half of 2004 and in 2005. It was the third Roland Berger study of its kind and shows changes in the restructuring patterns through the years. The article introduces the key results of this survey. In the survey, Germany is compared with the other European countries, primarily relative to the following issues: crisis reaction times, success factors in restructuring, methods of workforce reduction, early warning systems, financing and restructuring as on-going tasks. The article covering the subject "distressed debt" presents the current status and future trends from the banks' point of view. The study is based on the results of interviews conducted with 60 German banks in 2005, focusing on the following aspects: general distressed debt information, current status of the distressed debt market in Germany, overall conditions of the German distressed debt market and operation implementation or transaction costs.

– *Part 3* provides an introduction to the practical implementation of financial restructuring based on five examples. These case studies, which are described in an anonymous format as requested by the managing directors/board members involved, cover a broad industry spectrum: a manufacturer of specialty pharmaceuticals and diagnosis products, a production solicitation trading company for hardware and hardware systems, an output solutions (copying, printing, faxing, archiving) and presentation technology business, a wind power equipment assembly and sales organization offering a project development and service portfolio, as well as a plastics and furniture functionality technology company. Principally, the case studies first describe the initial situation at the beginning of the restructuring measures. Subsequently, experiences in terms of the transferability and applicability of financial restructuring, and thus the recapitalization approach are discussed.

As editors we hope that this book will contribute to the current discussion of the changing processes in the areas of restructuring and recapitalization, as well of their interfaces. It would please us immensely if our articles would serve as a reference work and source of ideas for our target group of experienced professionals.

Michael Blatz
Sascha Haghani
Karl-J. Kraus

Berlin, Düsseldorf
February 2006

TABLE OF CONTENTS

Part 1: The Success Factors of Restructuring in Germany – New Challenges for Corporate Financing

Innovative Crisis Management Concepts – An Up-to-Date Status Evaluation

Michael Blatz, Sascha Haghani

1   Preamble

Crises that threaten the very existence of a company can hit them all: medium-sized companies, or multinationals, corporations with or without a big name or famous brands, businesses of any size and in every industry. The headlines of the financial press announced bad news affecting a whole slew of prominent crisis candidates in 2004/2005, including KarstadtQuelle, Agfa Photo or Salamander. While public interest focuses on these spectacular cases, a large number of companies are fighting their final battle for survival in quiet oblivion. Although for the first time since 1999, Germany saw a slight decrease in corporate insolvencies in the first half of 2005, the absolute figures still paint a depressing picture; according to Creditreform estimates, close to 40,000 businesses will have to initiate insolvency proceedings in 2005. However, the insolvency applications constitute only the tip of the iceberg, given that this figure reflects only those companies whose continued existence is being acutely jeopardized by their inability to pay creditors. A much larger number of companies is battling strategic issues, results issues, or liquidity issues, and is thus latently at risk of becoming insolvent. A total of 270,000 companies are estimated to be in this situation.

The filing of an insolvency application marks only the final step on the path to ruin. Insolvency is not something that happens overnight, it usually takes quite some time to develop. Before a company has to make its way to the district court, it will generally have passed through three consecutive crisis phases. A typical crisis process begins with a strategy crisis. It is apparent in a company's failure to secure long-term success potential and attain strategic goals. The company's competitive standing in the market declines. Failure to successfully implement corrective action will sooner or later bring the company to an earnings crisis:[1] profit and profitability goals are not met. The company suffers from losses during reporting periods, which force it to delve into or use up its equity capital to the point where over-indebtedness looms. Unfortunately there are many practical examples of companies whose management teams repeatedly apply hide-your-head-in-the-sand policies, even to escalated earnings crisis scenarios, and fail to implement coun-

---

[1]   Success and profit crisis are sometimes being used synonymously.

termeasures. Under these circumstances the company cannot help but end up in a liquidity crisis, evident either in impending or actual insolvency. Nevertheless, reality doesn't always follow the script of contemporary crisis evolution: sometimes it skips individual phases, as it did in the case of Metallgesellschaft AG in 1994, when the company instantly fell into a liquidity crisis after misguided financial actions with derivates.[2] Smaller companies run a particularly high risk of being swallowed by a liquidity crisis/insolvency given their usual thin equity capital blanket – for example if a customer defaults on a large receivable.

The earlier an impending crisis is discovered and counter-acted, the larger the available action radius, and the higher the probability that the countermeasures introduced will succeed. In other words, the sooner a diagnosis is performed, the better the chances of successful therapy. This experience is confirmed in restructuring cases on a recurring basis, and is probably indisputable. However, it is indeed a problem that many a crisis develops quietly and frequently goes unnoticed by the affected company. In the earlier part of a crisis phase, the symptoms are less evident. To recognize strategic crises management must have very strong antennae that can pick up weak signals, such as unbalanced product/corporate portfolios, wrong investment decisions, changes in demand patterns, etc. In a strategic crisis, however, executive management frequently does not feel any adverse pressure, given that operationally, the business is still producing positive results. On the contrary, in the event of an earnings crisis, (and even more so once the company has entered a liquidity crisis), the crisis signals are usually so strong that they can no longer be ignored. In the late phases of the crisis, the action radius is, however, already extremely restricted, while the pressure to take action and the complexity of tasks increases simultaneously.

These correlations clearly demonstrate the importance of identifying crisis indicators early on. Consequently, Roland Berger Strategy Consultants has developed two effective early crisis detection tools, the "Integral approach to early crisis detection" and "Industry tracking":

- The weak point of conventional statistically/quantitatively oriented methods of early crisis detection is that they are primarily based on figures provided by the company that are sometimes doubtful, occasionally made to look better than reality, and that they are always retrospective. Market development and the company's environment are not even taken into account. An integral approach to early detection, however, requires that the company be analyzed in a market and industry context. This is a prerequisite for recording the exogenous and endogenous influences and their interaction in relation to the company's progress. The integral approach to early crisis detection developed by Roland Berger Strategy Consultants (RBSC) meets this standard. It was created using data from 70 case studies, which were chosen from more

---

[2]   See detailed background information in Goller (2000), page 137ff.

than 1,500 restructuring projects in a multistage selection process. One of the primary characteristics of the approach is that it provides an integral diagnosis and measurement system for early detection, through the combination of quantitative and qualitative methods. Its tools allow businesses to determine whether they are already in the middle of a strategic crisis: in a first step the system evaluates what root cause (for example value chain configuration, rapid growth, technology and fashion cycles) is responsible for a possible strategic corporate crisis. To determine this, the company is allocated to a specific cluster. In a second step, standardized questions and analysis instruments (such as SWOT analysis, structure/process analysis) can then be used to diagnose the existence and scope of this crisis; and the first steps toward elimination can be initiated.

- Industry tracking is the second tool available: the development of 14 industries, or more than 1,000 potential crisis companies and other companies in the German-speaking countries that turn over at least EUR 100 million p.a. is being monitored continually for an extended period. To this end companies are allocated to the various crisis phases based on the aforementioned crisis process. The result is illustrated in a "crisis clock" that divides the respective industry into various phases.

Threat detected – threat averted!? – In the case of corporate crises this simple formula unfortunately does not apply. The early recognition of a crisis does not ensure that restructuring will be successful; it merely increases the potential for recovery. Overcoming a company crisis or averting a looming insolvency are two of the most difficult management challenges a business may face. There is no patent recipe that guarantees a 100% success rate when it comes to revitalizing a business and leading it into a sustainable profit zone. Each restructuring case is different, every company has its own issues and each stakeholder aims at other interests in different situations. Although the heterogeneous nature and complexity of each individual case does not allow the utilization of standard solutions, some basic rules can be applied to the structure and content of restructuring concepts. The chance of a successful turnaround is greatly increased through compliance with these basic rules. They are outlined in the integral Roland Berger approach for restructuring companies in crisis, which will be discussed in detail in the following section.

The aforementioned uniqueness of each corporate crisis and the entirely different overall conditions that apply to each individual restructuring case have made it necessary to continuously update the RBSC approach to restructuring: in addition to the traditional methodology we have repeatedly pursued new paths in crisis management. These innovative approaches have been reflected from an academic perspective in ten dissertations and research projects.[3] These findings are now providing an important foundation for daily practical work at client sites. In section 3 of this article we will briefly introduce some of these innovative approaches to corporate financial restructuring. This focus is motivated by the fact that business recapitalization is gaining importance: companies who want to return to the path of growth after a successful reorganization and that bring the required potential to the table do not infrequently fail because of insufficient capital resources. This obstacle to growth must be removed by a new system of corporate financing.

2   The Traditional RBSC Approach to Restructuring

The literature discusses a wealth of differing phase models describing the restructuring process.[4] Despite their large number, theses phase models are very similar at the core. The primary objective of restructuring management is always to ensure the survival of the company in the short term and to reestablish competitiveness. Drawing on the experience gained in more than 1,500 restructuring projects, and based on our earlier research, Roland Berger Strategy Consultants has developed an approach to overcoming corporate crises that is equal to this objective. This restructuring approach combines standardized elements with tailor-made solutions that allow us to take industry-specific and company-specific needs into account.

The approach calls for a two-phase process (see Fig. 1). In phase I (duration two to six weeks) the current status is assessed, a restructuring concept is compiled and a program for immediate measures is initiated ("quick wins"). Moreover, the implementation organization for the restructuring concept is created in this first phase. In phase II (duration about six months to two years) the concept is broken down into details and implemented.

---

[3]   Detailed information on these dissertations and research projects can be found in Bickhoff et al. (2004).

[4]   Alternatively, see also Böckenförde (1996), page 52ff.; Gless (1996), page 130f.; Gunzenhauser (1995), page 22; Hess/Fechner (1998), page 8ff.; Kall (1999), page 70ff.; Krummenacher (1981), page 100; Krystek (1987), page 91ff. Müller (1986), page 317ff.; Vogt (1999), page 62ff.

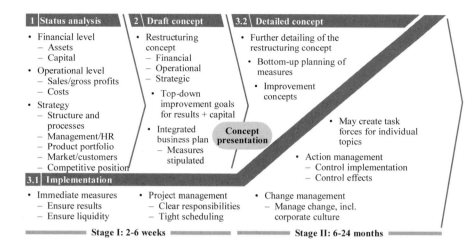

Fig. 1: The Roland Berger Strategy Consultants restructuring approach

The goal of the status assessment is to obtain a clear picture of the actual situation of the company. Effective measures can only be based on transparency. To achieve the latter, internal and external data is consolidated and analyzed. It is highly important for the status assessment to apply an adequate measure of precision and completeness, especially considering the time constraints that drive most crisis situations.

Based on this status assessment a rough draft of the restructuring concept is generated. It consists of three elements:

The first objective of *financial restructuring* is to take measures that avert the impending insolvency and that ensure the short-term survival of the business. This is the prerequisite for a sustainable restructuring process. The medium and long-term goal of financial restructuring is reestablishment of a healthy and solid capital structure.

In the course of *operational restructuring* measures required to improve the earnings and liquidity situation along the value chain are defined.

In addition to strategic reorientation of the company, *strategic restructuring* includes the structural and process-relevant (re)organization of the corporate units.

All of the effects of the measures planned in the restructuring concept are simultaneously consolidated in an integrated business plan with a time window of at least two years. The key elements of the plan are the P&L statement, balance sheet, and liquidity planning. The business plan provides the linkage between the three concept elements (financial and operational restructuring, as well as strategic reorientation) and serves as the basis for implementation monitoring. Given the time constraints, the concept must be designed as a rough concept from the outset.

Simultaneously with the compilation of the rough concept, the organizational requirements for implementation of the restructuring concept must already be put in place to ensure that immediate measures can be taken while the concept is being generated. The actual implementation process however does not begin until the shareholders have approved the restructuring concept, and if applicable, by the creditors. The implementation process is usually very complex. In some cases more than 1,000 individual steps must be defined, assessed, implemented and tracked in terms of financial efficacy. To achieve this, RBSC has developed the EDP tool, RBpoint, and the so-called restructuring scorecard – two instruments that help to reduce the complexity of the implementation process. Moreover, application of these tools allows immediate detection of deviations from the concept during the implementation process and the introduction of appropriate counter-measures. RBpoint supports the implementation process through a graphic control system and tracks the measures, particularly in terms of the time factor. Restructuring scorecards are dynamic monitoring instruments that track the sustainability of the initiated restructuring measures in terms of financial efficacy and goal attainment.

3   Innovative Ways out of Crisis Situations

The RBSC restructuring approach has a proven practical track record in terms of corporate crisis management. In the following chapter we will introduce four innovative methods that can lead companies out of crisis situations. These methods should be viewed as components of the integral Roland Berger approach described here. They are thus not implemented parallel to the conventional concept, but constitute components of strategic, operational, or financial restructuring projects in individual cases. Whether, and to what extent, these new methods are applied depends on the specific problems, the initial situation, and the concrete overall conditions of the respective restructuring scenario.

3.1   Recapitalization – Balance Sheet Cleanup, Decreased Interest Load and Preparation for Growth

Hard operational restructuring and reengineering have left deep marks in the balance sheets of many companies: high third party liabilities, low equity capital ratios, sometimes excessive book values, and a lack of liquid resources, which have largely been consumed during the implementation of the operational restructuring concept. One of the effects of high liabilities is an enormous amount of interest to be paid, which hinders or even prevents the company's growth. More-over, unfavorable balance sheet ratios make the company unattractive to potential (merger) partners. Funding requests for essential growth investments are rejected by the banks, and financing based on the company's own strength is only rarely an option. Thus such companies are frequently barred from entering a course of sus-tained reorientation.

One alternative to solve this problem is an integrated recapitalization concept that creates the required financial power to ensure competitiveness and growth – two of the prerequisites for a company's long-term survival. Recapitalization usually goes hand in hand with successful operational restructuring and aims at:

- Provision of new funding (fresh money)
- Relieving the pressure on balance sheet and earnings
- Stabilizing the financing circle
- Participation of the financing circle in the success of the company
- Paving the way for strategic cooperation

A heterogeneous financing circle representing diverging stakeholder interests and objectives is often the starting point for recapitalization. Consequently, providing credit institutions and banks with the option to continue to participate in, or with-draw from further funding is one of the key elements of recapitalization. To this end, the basic logic of recapitalization is:

- Fresh money is more valuable than existing commitments
- Withdrawal of individual institutions is (usually) only possible with a write-down
- Any write-down secured through a withdrawal depends on the asset class and benefits the company
- Those credit institutions that continue to provide financing participate in the company's success and have the opportunity to recover a portion/all of their receivables

Traditionally, recapitalization comprises four phases, but there can be some back and forth between individual phases (especially B and C) (see Fig. 2).

Fig. 2: The four (interdependent) phases of a recapitalization

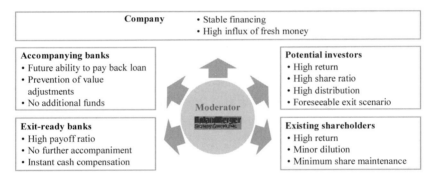

Fig. 3: Moderation and coordination of differing interests

Although the recapitalization logic based on the process as shown in the four-phase model may appear to be simplistic at first glance, it frequently poses enormous challenges for the company affected. The differing interests of the parties involved require a lot of moderation and coordination (see Fig. 3). This coordination of interests and financial tools is one of the key aspects that differentiate recapitalization from purely financially motivated solution approaches.

Depending on the enterprise-specific objective of recapitalization, various tools are integrated. A wholesaler in the southern part of Germany, for example, chose a combination of a capital cut with a subsequent cash capital increase, re-purchase of loans, debt-to-equity swaps, convertible profit participation certificates, and variable (result-dependent) interest elements. This allowed significant reduction of third party liabilities and interest while simultaneously providing funding for additional domestic and international growth. Moreover, the company's rating was considerably improved. The wholesaler was able to strengthen the firm's market position and return to profitable growth. The reduced financing circle now participates in the company's success to some extent. It took ten months from rough concept to technical implementation – time invested that certainly paid off.

3.2 Reaping the Profits of a (Self-Initiated) Industry Consolidation

The decline in demand caused by hesitant buying patterns and the intensified pressure on pricing due to fiercer competition (which is increasingly being internationalized), confront German companies with huge challenges. Even after years of successful operational restructuring and despite their partially optimized value chain processes, businesses in this country are forced to identify and realize further cost savings potentials in global competition. A prevalent self-initiated industry consolidation aims at overcoming scenarios that keep companies lagging just one step behind at all times, and to secure a competitive edge. To succeed, however, extensive strategic measures must be undertaken.

The essential effects that translate into acceptable profits in the short term can frequently only be attained through size advantages (for example, improved purchasing terms, risk control, better marketing positioning in the eyes of customers, etc.) and synergy effects. They can be achieved primarily through corporate mergers, and in some cases also through cooperation (e.g. purchasing cooperation). Given that this process also leads to a decrease in the number of firms in the market, this approach is called "industry consolidation". Driving such industry consolidations in their own interest, delivers three important benefits for the companies involved:

1. The earlier discussed scale and synergy effects can be realized

2. Given that fewer firms are crowding the market, the competitive pressure – even the pressure they feel themselves – is reduced (especially in terms of prices/margins)

3. The intensified market concentration reduces the risk that new local and international competitors will be added to those already present in the market[5]

---

[5] Measured based on the concentration measurement according to Lorenz, which describes the ratio of revenue shares and company size share. It is being assumed that the higher the concentration, the less attractive a start-up market entry. This does not preclude a market entry through a (hostile) takeover.

12

From the companies' point of view, various versions of industry consolidation are feasible:

1. The first version involves one firm in an industry taking the driving role by acquiring one or more companies for subsequent integration. This can either be an established local company or a new international competitor who uses this strategy to develop a new market.

2. In the second version, enterprises interested in industry consolidation get together and consolidate their businesses in a newly established holding company. Existing shareholders receive shares in this holding as compensation (for example in the ratio of the shares they bring to the table). The synergy potential realized in this scenario depends on the specific circumstances. Nevertheless, it frequently does not attain the scope realized in version 1.

3. A third possible (false) version of industry consolidation has the stakeholder companies entering into cooperative agreements. Although this frequently leads to the establishment of new companies and/or mergers (such as those to obtain shares in a mutually established purchasing organization), the key structures (value chain, administration, etc.) of each cooperating company remain intact. The existing shareholders keep their stakes in the respective businesses.

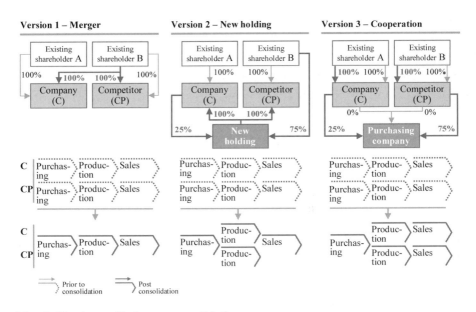

Fig. 4: Versions of industry consolidation

Before a company takes any steps toward industry consolidation it should consider two important questions: is our industry being affected by the consolidation? And if so, do we want to play an active or a passive role? Principally, it is advisable to take an active part in the process. It offers the company a better chance to realize its own interests and implement its visions. The decision as to which type of consolidation to select should be made depending on the individual scenario. Deciding factors are the resources available, time constraints, feasible synergy potentials, industry conditions, proprietorship issues, the speed at which decisions must be made, future responsibilities, etc.

During the phase of establishing contacts with possible merger candidates a high level of sensitivity is essential. Strategic motives are being disclosed and companies that still consider themselves competitors should be motivated to exchange sensitive information. In the contact establishment phase and during the initial legal execution (due diligence, contractual negotiations and execution of agreements) it is frequently absolutely necessary to involve an (external) coordinating agent, who enjoys the trust of all stakeholders, and who can, for example, assume the role of moderator and information pool for data exchange. Upon completion of the formal part of the integration, the operational integration must be pushed through as quickly as possible. Often outside assistance will also be required in this context.

Industry consolidation offers companies the option to again grow sustainably, even if the markets themselves are shrinking. Rooted in a strengthened home base, the corporation is then in a position to expand its international activities and to develop future markets for continued growth.

3.3 Corporate Restructuring – Creating Value Across All Corporate Divisions

Corporate restructuring is a solution for multinationals or larger companies who still achieve adequate consolidated results, but carry individual divisions with persistently negative or inadequate value contributions. The latter's bad performance is covered by the positive results of other units. This constellation is risky indeed, as these cross subsidies hamper the progress of the successful divisions, for example through misallocation of valuable top management resources, or the withdrawal of liquid funds. Moreover, due to increasing competitive pressure and the exacting demands of shareholders in relation to equity capital interest, all divisions are required to contribute to the growing value of the company. Only those who actually earn at least their capital cost – or that can attain this goal within a reasonable period of time, and at a tolerable expense – are taken into account when resources are allocated. All corporate activities must be evaluated in terms of value management criteria; and the outcome may make optimization of strategy and operational processes necessary. In this context, corporate restructuring provides an integral approach – from concept to implementation and ultimately, measurable results improvements.

Corporate restructuring begins with an assessment of the status quo – which divisions are contributing to the value of the company; and to what extent – or which divisions impact it adversely. Given the limited value of division results (e.g. smoothed over segment reporting due to allocations) and flexibility in the presentation of subsidiary results (e.g. for tax purposes), thorough analyses must be performed to evaluate the actual performance of business divisions and subsidiaries. This approach must include all parts of the group – strategic and operational levels, business divisions and central functions, controlling and executing units. Corporate restructuring comprises four levers:

1. Portfolio management

2. Value structure optimization

3. Optimization of corporate functions and

4. Operational performance management

These four levers are connected via a fifth element: control systems (see Fig. 5). To this end, the levers are not optimized separately; on the contrary, the interdependencies between levers are taken into account. In the case of portfolio decisions, for instance, potentials derived from operational performance improvement are considered.

The direct key objectives of corporate restructuring are:

- Creating an optimized business portfolio, resulting in good positioning of the individual business divisions on the market, achievement of consistently positive value contributions, and high synergy potentials between the divisions,

- Developing a powerful, optimally sized, organizational structure in relation to performance aspects, and an optimum level of centralization or decentralization based on the overall internal and external conditions,

- A depth-optimized value structure through targeted insourcing and outsourcing of business activities, and as a result, optimized utilization of resources (e.g. capital, management). This requires an improved linkage (material flow, information flow) of locations, know-how and skills, among other things.

- The increase in existing revenue, savings and liquidity reserves,

- The development of easily manageable control systems with a stronger focus and action orientation – this is, among other things, achieved through the streamlining/focusing and harmonization of existing reports and reporting structures, the introduction of cause-effect relations (for example scorecards), increased future orientation in reporting, and/or utilization of measures management tools within the scope of project work.

As a result, business activities are better bundled, complexities are reduced, reserves are increased, and the basis for future-focused growth is established.

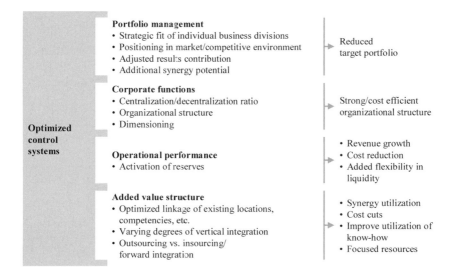

Fig. 5: The elements of corporate restructuring

3.4 Utilizing Insolvency as a Restructuring Opportunity

In the introduction we described insolvency as the last step following the three crisis phases. Trapped in a state of insolvency, the affected companies previously were often left with but a single option: stopping their entrepreneurial activities, and settling debts with creditors by selling any remaining assets. Statutory restructuring has been greatly improved by lawmakers with the insolvency statute reform (1999).[6] Pursuant to the reformed insolvency statute, the mutual satisfaction of creditors can be achieved through liquidation of the company, as well as through its continuation.[7] Contrary to the obsolete bankruptcy law, the idea of continuing the company, or parts thereof, is beginning to prevail, thanks to this new statute. According to the new statute, insolvency is no longer the end of it all; it can actually serve as a design tool and instrument in the restructuring option. In complete synchronicity with the "creative destruction" method hailed by Schumpeter, insolvency can, in certain cases, be understood as an opportunity to unload

---

[6]   Ref. Herzig (2001), page 339.

[7]   Ref. § 1 InsO.

16

old liabilities, change obsolete corporate structures, or alter the business direction. The new motto can thus be: emerge from insolvency as a stronger company.

In the event of continuation, the law provides the insolvent company with two or four different options: the insolvency plan (self-directed with prepackaged plan, or through a trustee with trustee plan), transferring the restructuring process either through transfer to a hive-off vehicle, or sale to a third party[8] (see Fig. 6).

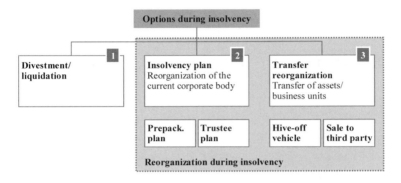

Fig. 6: Options in the event of insolvency

What opportunities are inherent in insolvency? The new insolvency statute provides significantly simpler processes for the core elements of restructuring.

- Staff reductions have, for example, been accelerated thanks to a restriction of termination periods to three months. The maximum severance package has also been limited to 2.5 monthly salaries, which allows processing in a single step.

- Thanks to insolvency gap subsidies, the company also attains significant liquidity relief for a period of three months.

- The only limited verification of the social choices also enables development of balanced staff structures.[9]

- The termination of – potentially cost-intensive company agreements – facilitates the process considerably.

---

8   Transferring reorganization calls for the transfer of a company, operation or part of an operation from the debtor to another already existing legal entity or one yet to be established. Ref. Balz/Landfermann (1999), page 131ff.

9   Applies in the event an agreement with the workers' council (WC) is reached: In the event no agreement with the WC can be reached within three weeks, proceedings with the German Labor Court are filed. The Federal Employment Office and the arbitration committee do not have to be involved.

- The insolvent company's right to choose which mutual contracts to fulfill brings relief from disadvantageous obligations; it can even bring cash flow relief. Particularly "old economy" companies are usually weighed down by significant pension obligations that are transferred to the pension insurance association in the event of insolvency. Long-term agreements (such as those for real estate) can be cleaned up and asset shifts that have an adverse effect on total assets can be revoked thanks to a special contestation law.

Prior to this quasi voluntary move into insolvency, it should however be investigated in minute detail whether the root cause of the corporate crisis is not for example a product portfolio that does not conform to the market, or an operational weakness. Moreover, the fact that a company is restructurable does not suffice; the company must also be worth restructuring. If this is not the case, or if the causes of the corporate crisis are operational inadequacies, restructuring on the basis of insolvency does not hold a lot of promise.

Thanks to the option to apply for insolvency early on, i.e. in the event of impending inability to pay, the new insolvency statute protects creditors from suffering continued damage. At the same time, introduction of the insolvency plan and self-administration provides the debtor with an opportunity to control the majority of the insolvency process, and maintain the asset or possibly continue to participate in later value gains. To this effect, the implementation must take place under enormous time constraints in the tug-of-war zone between legal and financial restrictions and the stakeholders' loss of trust. It is therefore imperative to create transparency quickly and to clearly show creditors where and how value gains can be achieved. This does not solely hinge on a stable financial concept, but also on the rigorous utilization of the proper process simplifications[10] and extensive communication[11] with external stakeholders and employees. However, if the implementation is carried out consistently, the respective company can unload oppressive old obligations and attain a considerably improved starting point.

4 Summary: Consolidate Quickly, Return to Growth Quickly

In addition to the traditional Roland Berger Strategy Consultants restructuring approach, Section 3 introduced four innovative ways out of corporate crisis sce-

---

[10] For a detailed description of restructuring in the insolvency phase, ref. Zirener (2004), page 139ff.

[11] For comments on communications during the restructuring process, ref. Buschmann (2004), page 197ff.

narios: recapitalization, industry consolidation, corporate restructuring, and utilization of insolvency as an opportunity. All four of these approaches share a common main goal: establishing an initial basis from which the company will attain profitable growth in the future.

- The goal of recapitalization is to clean up old obligations in the balance sheet and improve the results by reducing interest expenditures. Achieving this and injecting new resources removes the existing growth barrier. Based on this foundation, a balanced concept of contributions by, and opportunities for, all stakeholders must be moderated (recap concept).

- Industry consolidation aims at improving the competitive situation of the company considerably, especially through scale and synergy effects. On the basis of stronger competitive positioning, growth potential in the domestic and international markets can be developed with a much greater likelihood of success.

- The corporate restructuring approach better focuses corporate activities (business portfolio and value chain), while increasing reserves and using resources in a targeted manner. The benchmark for future growth is based on a clean slate.

- Restructuring during/from insolvency is another approach offering an opportunity of growth based on a clean slate. The companies involved can take advantage of the opportunity to cost-effectively free themselves from old obligations of all kinds (employees that are incapable or not motivated to do their jobs, contracts, business units, etc.). The firm can then plan its future on the basis of a healthy and growth-oriented core.

In our opinion, the creation of a basis for growth (frequently through an initial consolidation) and subsequent actual attainment of growth is the most promising strategy to again achieve sustainable success on the market (see Fig.7) and to increase the corporate value (see Fig. 8). In this context, significant consolidation at the beginning of the restructuring process is usually unavoidable.

(Formerly) crisis-ridden companies with a now positive ROI consolidate their revenues more often and more quickly than those with a negative ROI. In the course of reorientation, it is not a voluntary move for successful companies, but an obligation to re-grow sales in a sustainable manner. Many companies – especially those who proved not to be successful after their consolidation – are under the impression that restructuring ends with the cleaning up of revenues and costs and that it is then time to return to the status quo once again. The above graphic does, however, show that the – somewhat harsh – motto must be: grow or die. Mere consolidation will not suffice. Only sustained growth will return these companies to the path of profitable success. The results of the survey show that the 40 companies of the 102 businesses assessed that were able to launch new products attained long-term success in 77% of all cases. Those companies that were able to develop new markets enjoyed comparably good results: 74% achieved sustained success.

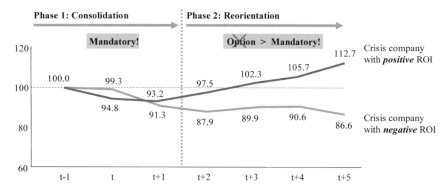

Fig. 7: Revenue development of 102 crisis companies over time

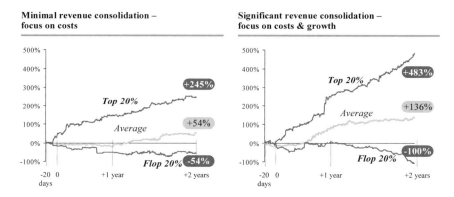

Fig. 8: Development of company value (excess return) in crisis companies that focus on costs, compared with those that focus on costs and growth[12]

Another Roland Berger survey[13] clearly indicates that development of company value in crisis companies (based on 40 crisis companies evaluated from 1993 to 2002) definitely correlates to the choice of restructuring program. Fig. 8 shows that at a rate of 54% growth the average development of risk adjusted earnings in businesses that merely consolidate lags significantly behind the results of those

---

[12]   Ref. Lafrenz (2004b), page 205.

[13]   Ref. Lafrenz (2004a).

companies, that in addition to focusing on consolidation, also placed emphasis on a parallel or subsequent growth strategy (average increase 136%).

Those enterprises in crisis that are indeed successful often secure financing via external capital influx, in particular also by way of a capital increase. Approximately three fourths of those businesses that were able to implement a capital increase in a time of crisis attained sustained positive results.

In summary, it has been established that at the core, restructuring always follows a similar path. In this context, the approach based on RBSC's integral restructuring concept has proven itself in practical application time and again. A number of crisis factors are nonetheless extremely situation-specific, especially given the fact that the corporate environment always develops dynamically. Therefore it is even more important to not rely on known and conventional methods exclusively, but to take innovative routes. This particularly includes a coherent financing concept that meets these dynamic requirements. After all, "Those who rest rust".

Bibliography

Ansoff, Igor H. (1976): Managing Strategic Surprise and Discontinuity: Strategic Response to Weak Signals. In: Zeitschrift für betriebswirtschaftliche Forschung, 28th year, 1976, pages 129-152.

Balz, Manfred/Landfermann, Hans-Georg, (1999): Die neuen Insolvenzgesetze. (The New Insolvency Statutes), Düsseldorf.

Bickhoff, Nils et al. (2004): Die Unternehmenskrise als Chance – Innovative Ansätze zur Sanierung und Restrukturierung. (Corporate Crisis as an Opportunity – Innovative Approaches to Recapitalization and Restructuring), Berlin a.o.

Böckenförde, Björn (1996): Unternehmenssanierung. (Corporate Restructuring) 2nd Printing, Stuttgart.

Buschmann, Holger (2004): Stakeholder-Management als notwendige Bedingungen für erfolgreiches Turnaround-Management. (Stakeholder Management as Essential Prerequisites of Successful Turnaround Management In: Bickhoff, Nils et al. (Editors): Die Unternehmenskrise als Chance – Innovative Ansätze zur Sanierung und Restrukturierung. (Corporate Crisis as an Opportunity – Innovative Approaches to Recapitalization and Restructuring), Berlin a.o., pages 197-220 .

Creditreform (2004): Insolvenzen, Neugründungen, Löschungen 1. Halbjahr 2004 (Insolvencies, New Companies Established, Companies Deleted 1st Half 2004), Internet: http://www.creditreform.de/angebot/analysen/0042/01.php, 2004.

Creditreform (Hrsg.) (2003): Insolvenzen, Neugründungen und Löschungen – Jahr 2003 (Insolvencies, New Companies Established, Companies Deleted – 2003), Neuss.

Gless, Sven-Eric (1996): Unternehmenssanierung: Grundlagen – Strategien – Maßnahmen. (Corporate Restructuring: Basics – Strategies – Measures), Wiesbaden.

Goller, Martin (2000): Aktuelle Vergleichsverfahren in Deutschland. (Current Composition Proceedings in Germany), Frankfort/Main a.o.

Gunzenhauser, Peter (1995): Unternehmenssanierung in den Neuen Bundesländern: Eine Untersuchung des Werkzeugmaschinenbaus (Corporate Restructuring in the New German Federal States: An Assessment of Tooling Machine Engineering), Cologne.

Hess, Harald/Fechner, Dietrich (1998): Sanierungshandbuch. 3. Auflage (Restructuring Manual, 3rd Printing, Neuwied a.o.

Kall, Florian (1999): Controlling im Turnaround-Prozeß: theoretischer Bezugsrahmen, empirische Fundierung und handlungsorientierte Ausgestaltung einer Controlling-Konzeption für den Turnaround-Prozeß. (Controlling in the Turnaround-Process: Theoretical Reference Frame, Empiric Foundation and Action-Oriented Approach to a Controlling Concept for the Turnaround Process), Frankfort/Main a.o.

Kraus, Karl-J./Gless, Sven-Eric (2004): Erstellung von Restrukturierungs-/ Sanierungskonzepten. In: Kraus, Karl-J./Blatz, Michael/Evertz, Derik et al. (Editors) Kompendium der Restrukturierung – erweiterter und ergänzter Sonderdruck aus Buth (Compendium of Restructuring – expanded and completed special excerpt from Buth), Andrea K./Hermanns, Michael (Editors): Restrukturierung, Sanierung und Insolvenz. (Restructing, Recapitalization and Insolvency) 2nd Printing, Munich, pages 17-50.

Krummenacher, Alfred (1981): Krisenmanagement: Leitfaden zum Verhindern und Bewältigen von Unternehmenskrisen. (Crisis Management: Guidelines for the Prevention and Overcoming of Corporate Crises), Zurich.

Krysteck, Ulrich (1987): Unternehmenskrisen: Beschreibung, Vermeidung und Bewältigung überlebenskritischer Prozesse in Unternehmungen. (Corporate Crises: Description, Prevention and Handling of Mission-Critical Processes in Companies), Wiesbaden.

Lafrenz, Karsten (2004a): Shareholder Value-orientierte Sanierung: Eine kapitalmarktorientierte Analyse des Einflusses von Krisensituationen und Handlungskonzeptionen auf den Sanierungserfolg. (Shareholder Value-Oriented Restructuring: A Capital Market Oriented Analysis of the Impact of Crisis Scenarios and Action Concepts on Restructuring Success), Wiesbaden.

Lafrenz, Karsten (2004b): Unternehmenswertsteigerung durch Restrukturierung. (Corporate Value Increase Through Restructuring) In: Kraus, Karl-J./Blatz, Michael/Evertz, Derik et al. (Editors): Compendium of Restructuring – expanded and completed special excerpt from Buth, Andrea K./Hermanns, Michael (Editors): Restructuring, Recapitalization and Insolvency. 2nd Printing, Munich, pages 193-213.

Müller, Rainer (1986): Krisenmanagement in der Unternehmung: Vorgehen, Maßnahmen und Organisation. (Crisis Management in Corporations: Approach, Measures and Organization, 2nd Printing, Frankfort/Main a.o.

Roland Berger Strategy Consultants (Editors) (2001): Stürmische Zeiten meistern – Erfolgreiche Restrukturierung von Unternehmen, (Mastering Stormy Days – Successful Corporate Restructuring, Survey.

Roland Berger Strategy Consultants (2004): Alle Kräfte wecken. (Awakening All Powers) In: Capital 2004, no. 25, pages 85-86 based on the RBSC survey: Managing for Growth.

Vogt, Matthias (1999): Sanierungsplanung: Eine Darstellung innerhalb und außerhalb des Insolvenzrechts. (Planning for Restructuring: A View from Within and Without the Insolvency Law), Wiesbaden.

Zirener, Jörg (2004): Sanierung in der Insolvenz – Ansätze zum Wert erhaltenden Einsatz des Insolvenzverfahrens. (Restructuring During Insolvency). In: Bickhoff, Nils et al. (Editors): Corporate Crisis as an Opportunity – Innovative Approaches to Recapitalization and Restructuring), Berlin a.o., pages 139-165.

Corporate Restructuring in Germany – The Economy Remains Tense, but Restructuring Offers Definite Opportunities

Bernd Brunke, Stephan Foerschle, Sascha Haghani, Florian Huber, Nils von Kuhlwein, and Björn Waldow

1 The State of the German Economy

The German economy remains tense. Overall prosperity is on the decline and the country is losing its competitive edge – both compared with the other EU member states, as well as leading industrialized nations, such as the United States and Japan. Since 2003 per capita gross domestic product has fallen below the EU15 average. In 2004, at a rate of approximately EUR 27,800 it was only slightly above the EU25 of about EUR 25,700 per capita. The unemployment rate has been rising simultaneously (well above 10%) as has the national debt. Moreover, Germany shows the weakest economic growth in all of Europe. The average annual growth rate between 2001 and 2004 averages less than 1%.

In the international comparison, Europe lags behind as a whole. From a global perspective, the continent's economy grew at the slowest rate. In its search for future growth opportunities, the world economy is increasingly focusing on Asia. Asia's gross domestic product is estimated to increase by 7 to 8% per annum by 2008. The EU25's comparative value, on the other hand, is only about 2% per year.

Moreover, EU enlargement poses enormous challenges for Germany due to a huge gap in terms of human resource costs and average hours worked. New EU members, such as Poland and Slovakia boast hourly wages that are 80 to 90% below those paid in Germany. At the same time, workers in these countries put in 30 to 40% more hours per year.

In addition to these mostly intra-European issues, looking at the big picture, advancing globalization is compelling Germany (and almost every other highly evolved industrial nation in Europe) to make adjustments. Many companies increasingly find themselves confronted with globally active competitors in their domestic markets (see Fig. 1).

Fig. 1: Virtually all industries find themselves confronted with tighter market conditions and an increased risk of exposure to corporate crises

Location-specific growth impediments frequently go hand in hand with the challenges of global competition. This is especially true for Germany with its dense network of rules and regulations, or its present form of workers' participation.

Given this background it is hardly surprising that the number of corporate insolvencies in Germany has posted historical record highs in the past several years. In 2004, Germany came in second in Europe with 39,600 companies filing for bankruptcy protection. This translates into 135 out of every 10,000 German companies having to initiate insolvency proceedings in 2004. Only France, which saw 40,042 company insolvencies during the same period, outperformed Germany in this respect.[1]

While the 0.3% increase in insolvencies from 2003 to 2004 was considerably smaller than the 4.9% that rattled the nation from 2002 to 2003, this certainly is no indication that the trend will turn around any time soon. According to Creditreform estimates the damage inflicted and that will be inflicted on the German economy by these bankruptcies total around EUR 39.4 billion for 2004 alone. The number of employees displaced by the insolvency of their employer is estimated to total about 600,000.

What is striking about this scenario is that although the spectacular cases, such as Holzmann, Babcock, Kirch, or Walter-Bau, are the ones making the headlines in the financial press, small and medium-sized companies are increasingly in trouble also. Creditreform cites a lack of collateral and equity capital as the key reason for these problems. The minimal equity capital held by German medium-sized businesses, which averages around 7.5% of the balance sheet total, is not only at the

---

[1] Source: Creditreform (http://www.creditrefom.de/angebote/analysen/ 0047/02. php; called up on September 3, 2005).

low end of the scale in European and international comparisons, but it is also a far cry from the 30% that is considered as stable equity capitalization by most financial institutions and investors.

This corresponds with the results of the quarterly industry tracking record compiled by Roland Berger comprising 1,000 German companies. It indicates that at this time, about 40% of all companies in Germany are showing signs of a strategic crisis, earnings crisis, and/or liquidity crisis (see Fig. 2).

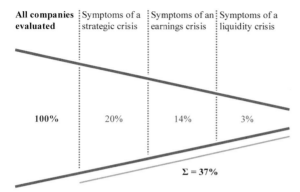

Fig. 2: Classification of companies by crisis status

Based on these circumstances, approximately EUR 100 to 150 billion in corporate loans in Germany can be categorized as so-called "problem loans" or "non-performing loans". This estimate is based on an analysis performed by large German banks that tag about 4 to 5% of their corporate loans as "distressed debt" or "bad loans".

In recent years, this scenario has attracted specialized, mostly Anglo-American turnaround investors. Many renowned German companies were targeted and the first transactions have already been completed. Advent, Apax, Blackstone, Candover, Cinven, KKR, Providence, Saban Capital, or Texas Pacific, and many others have already invested billions of euros into German corporations: Celanese, Kabel Deutschland, Brenntag, ProSieben, Premiere, BertelsmannSpringer, Viterra Energy, Dynamit Nobel, Friedrich Grohe, Auto-Teile-Unger (A.T.U.) are among the prominent examples. In particular the high accruals and write-downs that German banks have undertaken or have had to undertake, in the past few years, as well as the fact that the equity capital guidelines stipulated by Basel II are much more stringent for problem loans, may result in the continued willingness of many banks to sell a portion of their non-performing loans to these distressed debt investors at relatively high discounts on the nominal loan value. This increases the chances of investors to participate over-proportionally in potential value gains attained through restructuring.

2 Restructuring Under the New German Insolvency Law – Beggars Still Can't Be Choosers

When Germany's new Insolvency Law came into force five years ago, legislators had two goals in mind. First, the new law was intended to harmonize and modernize the legal situation. Second, it was to foster a new "insolvency culture" centered around the notion of facilitating a fresh start.

At last, debtors would cast off the traditional role of rogues who were beneath the law – a role that, successive amendments notwithstanding, had weighed on them since the first German bankruptcy law was decreed in 1794.

The revamped legislation was modeled partly around key aspects of the USA's Chapter 11 proceedings:

1. The option of filing for insolvency early on, i.e. when insolvency for lack of liquidity is imminent but there is still sufficient cash and free collateral to keep the business afloat.

2. The option of devising an insolvency plan together with the main stakeholders to keep the company alive, free from legacy burdens and existing obligations. The goal is to enable it to pay off its debts over time and thus help creditors recover more of their assets.

3. The option of control staying in the hands of the debtor, i.e. that the existing management – ostensibly the people with the most experience of the situation – continue to run the business, subject to court and trustee supervision.

From a restructuring angle, all three goals marked a step in the right direction. The ongoing Roland Berger restructuring survey identified three factors that can make or break a restructuring exercise:

1. The problem must be recognized as soon as the company has slipped into an earnings crisis, that is before it gets into a real liquidity crunch.

2. A comprehensive set of actions must eliminate all the causes of crisis, signaling to stakeholders that there are sound prospects for successful continuation.

3. The management, assisted by relevant experts, should be the key knowledge resource in the design and realization of restructuring.

Precisely for this reason, it is vital to accurately read the signs emanating from the latest statistics – and from our own hands-on experience.

But imminent illiquidity, valid as grounds for insolvency under the new law, is almost completely irrelevant. Insolvency plans are drawn up in just 0.3% of all cases. Continued management by the debtor is an extremely rare exception.

Though many and varied, the reasons for this situation can, in our experience, roughly be summarized as follows.

We have found that companies still act too late because of the stigma attached to managers who file for insolvency. Many managers are reluctant to leverage insolvency as a way to gain room to breathe and make a fresh start. When the last asset is under lien and the last receivable assigned, however, there is usually too little substance left for a turnaround under protection of insolvency.

Trustees, bankers and other stakeholders often consider the procedure for drawing up insolvency plans as too complex. Content is not the main issue here: Even out-of-court restructuring can reach similar levels of complexity. It is the red tape surrounding planning approval that can artificially bloat the stakeholder community and make the whole venture unmanageable. What is more, many creditors still prefer to quickly sell off bits of the company (witness Babcock Borsig, Kirch and Walter Bau) to at least achieve partial satisfaction immediately. They shy away from satisfaction in installments paid out of free cashflow because they consider the risk over time as too high.

Similarly, creditors frequently indulge an unjustified mistrust toward the former management and are loath to leave them holding the reins. Painful experience of corporate malpractice has made matters worse.

Despite such discouraging experience, there are clear signs that change is indeed on the way, albeit more slowly than had perhaps been hoped.

Since the new law was introduced, the number of insolvency applications refused for lack of assets has declined noticeably, dropping by up to 40%. In special cases, insolvency plans have been used – particularly in situations where the business model requires a special legal status that would be removed in the event of a sale. The fact that creditors' committees are rejecting more and more administrators can be seen as another clear indication that the procedural power base is shifting.

We expect to see these trends firm up in the future. International and interdisciplinary collaboration will play an important part in keeping complex rescue procedures manageable. Especially cross border cases like Eurofood, which is discussed under the EU Insolvency regulation, will foster this development further.

Despite all the caveats, examples such as Babcock Borsig and Kirch Media demonstrate the considerable capabilities of German insolvency law as it stands. In these cases, the astute sale of healthy units has enabled even major corporate insolvencies to be brought to successful conclusions. The return from rogues to riches can indeed be real and rapid.

3 Distressed Capital – The Future of Corporate Financing in Germany?

Over the past five years, an increasing number of established companies have been facing growing challenges: Rising leverages, decreasing equity ratios and increasing financing costs due to deteriorating credit ratings combined with additional financing needs for restructuring and growth investments, as well as internationalization pressure. Companies are not only facing strategic crises, but also profit and liquidity crises. These challenges represent a dilemma for these companies. They need new capital, but access to capital is increasingly difficult.

In recent years shareholders and existing lenders have not met the need for capital. This is reflected in a drop in equity ratios and a downward trend in book loan extensions by German banks. Reasons for this include stricter credit assessments as a result of Basel II, and are highlighted by terms such as "fair value" and "recoverable amount" as well as the end of government guaranties for public banks in 2005.

Distressed companies are asking how they can obtain corporate financing for long-term survival. An analysis of the German market may provide the answer.

Financial investors in Germany have been operating in the German market as distressed capital investors for several years. They offer companies an alternative form of corporate financing. What does distressed capital mean? Distressed capital refers to all purchases of titles in and claims to distressed companies. Private equity companies specializing in distressed companies buy company equity. In contrast, distressed debt investors generally purchase loans, bonds or uncertificated claims. In this case, distressed debt refers to non-performing bank loans – corporate or real estate loans – extended to customers.

The strategies of distressed investors can be classified as being active or passive. These strategies are different in the level of influence that can be exerted on business activities and management as well as in providing additional funds. Due to funding needs, only active investment strategies are conceivable for corporate financing that create a controlling position and lead to an active influence on business policies. This is accompanied by an injection of additional liquidity.

Borders between private equity and distressed debt investors are blurred. The purchase of payables by debt investors is followed by a debt-equity swap so that investors can take ownership of the company. The entry points are different, but the goals are the same. Financial investors proceed under the following conditions: favorable market position and good performance in the core business, poor results, relatively high funding needs as well as a short time horizon to turnaround. It is necessary to analyze the development of both markets in Germany in order to forecast the future development of distressed capital.

According to the Association of German Private Equity Companies, gross investments in the private equity market in 2004 amounted to EUR 3.8 billion. Less than 1% of these investments were for turnaround investments. The maximum gross investments in distressed companies amounted to 1.7% in 2001. Turnaround equity can therefore still be considered a niche market. It does not yet represent a form of established corporate financing. The low number and cautious approach of the players also indicates that there are still barriers between investors and companies. German turnaround funds such as CMP, Orlando, Nordwind Capital und Equatis are still young and their fund volume relatively low. Furthermore, they still have to demonstrate successes. Several investors such as Alchemy and Clayton Dubilier & Rice withdrew from the market after initial exposure. Other investors such as Questor and Electra have not yet made a big splash. On the other hand, investors such as Cerberus and Bridgepoint are starting to focus on the German market.

According to various analyses, the German market potential for distressed debt is estimated at EUR 100-320 billion. In 2003, the transaction volume amounted to EUR 3 billion. In 2005, a volume of EUR 20 billion is expected. However, these volumes generated by past transactions were mainly the result of portfolio trades. Portfolio trades are sales of entire portfolios of non-performing bank loans, preferably with real estate collateral. Exceptions to this are sales of single-name distressed corporate loans. The strategies behind portfolio trades include taking over loan servicing and repayment, disposing of or auctioning off collateralized real estate as well as purchasing various portfolios to generate bundling effects and capital market placement. Only active strategies with influence and control can be considered for corporate loans. Investors such as Cerberus and Lone Star, investment banks such as Goldman Sachs and Morgan Stanley, and increasingly commercial banks, such as Deutsche Bank, are entering the market. So far, investors have been selective in the corporate loan segment due to the fact that greater expertise and capacities are required. Recent transactions include IhrPlatz, Georg von Opel and KarstadtQuelle. It can be expected that investments in rewarding opportunities will rise.

It is obvious that there is a shift in paradigms: Distressed capital investors are assuming the role of traditional lenders. However, distressed capital is still in its infancy. What is the reason for this?

The political and statutory framework is more of an obstacle than an investment-promoting factor. Restrictive dismissal protection for employees and the powerful position of workers' councils in Germany prevent taking quick action and making capacity adjustments. Major bureaucracy and high non-wage labor costs are also a consideration. A big coalition government does not bring much hope of eliminating uncertainties in tax legislation.

Management quality is perceived as a barrier. Anglo-American investors criticize German management as not having the right qualifications for professional restructuring and that not enough emphasis is placed on value creation. Due to a lack of experience, investors in Germany do not have any capable local turnaround managers who can be relied on for successful restructuring. Slow restructuring implementation impedes the expected return on investments.

Cultural barriers also play a role. A regular complaint includes German management and employee risk aversion and the conservative approach of banks during a workout. Furthermore, as shown during the "locust" debate, financial investors are not necessarily welcome in Germany.

Finally, Germany's relatively underdeveloped financial market orientation is another important reason. Furthermore, discussions on placing legal restrictions on investment activities have made investors cautious.

The entry of financial investors is impacting corporate restructuring. Restructuring goals are shifting away from damage control, repaying loan principal and eliminating the crises causes and are moving toward maximizing returns instead. This means a strong focus on cash and ensuring medium-term divestments in terms of an exit strategy. In the future, the best restructuring option will be selected based on individual situations. Restructuring will be primarily managed by restructuring consultants due to a lack of detailed market know-how and investor relations as well as absent management. This way, investors can ensure the preparation and speedy implementation of an ambitious 100-day program.

In conclusion, three hypotheses can be stated regarding future development:

1. Distressed capital will establish itself as a stable part of corporate financing in Germany within the next five years

   The players will continue to be selective in their investments. But three prerequisites can increase access to distressed capital:

   - Promoting an efficient market solution. The lack of an efficient market solution for corporate financing is still holding back the German market. Greater capital market orientation such as found in the American financial system would lead to a broader financing base for companies. Furthermore, a developed secondary market for debt titles would enable quick exits from investments and provide for greater fungibility. Common platforms for comparing supply and demand would create transparency, and players could contribute their know-how in line with their competencies.

   - Reducing political and legal obstacles. Germany must improve its international competitiveness in the short and long term. Germany has the highest income tax burden in Europe. Its non-wage labor costs are just as unsavory to investors as are its restrictive dismissal protection laws and the powerful position of workers' councils. Distressed investments in Germany were also promoted by American-influenced insolvency rules.

In Germany, prepackaged plans are still greeted with only limited acceptance. Rules on substituting equity during reorganization and assignment of bank loans only upon debtor consent inhibit flexibility during insolvency. In contrast, in the US there are debt-oriented rules based on a going-concern approach, giving distressed investments higher priority over existing collateral. The prepackaged plan is the dominant approach in insolvencies, which enables influencing by way of blocking positions.

- Change in mentality. All players in Germany must change their mindset in terms of corporate financing. Investors must be perceived as an opportunity and not as a threat for companies. This would create a productive climate for exchanging information and not scare off potential investors.

All players involved profit from distressed capital

Investments in these companies and successful restructuring means everyone wins. Companies get a new chance and avoid obstacles due to conflicting interests among the financing banks. Banks can improve their cash position and ROE. At the same time, they reduce their risks and losses. Investors can realize profitable returns by involving experienced restructuring experts and implementing their strategies. Employees can also profit from investor involvement, as company survival means most of the jobs are saved and rewarding compensation systems can be implemented. Restructuring experts benefit as turnaround management can generate profits through their company holdings and restructuring consultants can enjoy success-related bonuses.

Future development will lead to a convergence between investor groups and industry consolidation

A convergence between distressed equity, distressed debt investors and specialized commercial banks will occur. The former differs from the debt investors in their entry point into the company. However, their strategic goals are the same. The investor groups must bundle their specific know-how in order to create an effective market solution in light of declining returns. Bundling competencies will lead to increased efficiencies and margins.

Ultimately, an investor-driven consolidation of the various industries is expected. Investors will bundle investments together according to industry (total industry solutions) and thereby generate higher returns.

Distressed capital will ultimately become accepted in Germany. Overall, investors are very professional and aim to add value and provide corporate stability.

4 Restructuring Success Factors

Restructuring can yield considerable opportunities – as evidenced by Roland Berger Strategy Consultants based on an analysis of the 2003 annual report data of more than 500 large German corporations. The analysis showed that all of these German companies could increase their consolidated earnings before interest and tax (EBIT) by about EUR 40 billion, if they were in a position to increase their return on sales to their respective industry average. If they were actually able to attain values comparable to those of the respective top 20% of their industry, the potential gains would be significantly higher – about EUR 280 billion. Considering these figures, it is hardly surprising that the German distressed and turnaround financing market is highly attractive for domestic as well as international investors.

Integral restructuring of the affected company, however, is the key prerequisite for realization of such potential value increases. In the context of the restructuring concept, two basic issues must be examined:

- How can short-term survival of the company be ensured?

- How can competitiveness be ensured and expanded sustainably?

Based on the experience gathered in more than 1,500 restructuring projects since 1990, Roland Berger Strategy Consultants has developed an integral restructuring approach that consolidates these aspects into one concept and quantifies them in integrated P&L, balance sheet, and cash flow planning (see Fig. 3).

Fig. 3: The Roland Berger Strategy Consultants restructuring triangle

The focus of operational restructuring is initially placed on securing the company at risk's short-term survival by taking quick actions to shore up the company's cash position and improve results. In the medium and long term, a business impacted by crisis will only be able to regain its competitiveness if it solves its self-made problems, eliminates operational process deficits, and positions itself in the market and competitive environment with a keen eye on the future. This is where strategic restructuring begins. Financial restructuring, which often goes hand in hand with active recapitalization, puts the final prerequisites in place for adequate equity capital and cash flow to fund future profitable growth.

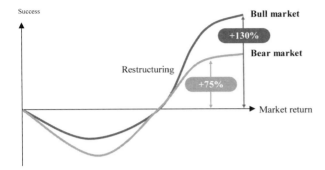

Fig. 4: Development of successful restructuring cases in bull and bear markets

Based on a survey of approx. 1,000 German companies listed on the stock market, Roland Berger Strategy Consultants was able to show that even in a bear market earnings of more than 75% (after risk adjustment) above the market average (represented by the CDAX Index) are absolutely feasible. In a bull market the value could actually be around 130% above average market returns (see Fig. 4). Nevertheless, this hinges on an all-encompassing approach to restructuring as explained above.

The analyses have also revealed that restructuring is particularly successful if three basic rules are observed in the described integral restructuring approach:

1. First consolidate!
   Consolidation through workforce reduction, site closings, decreased material costs, relocation of production, streamlining hierarchical structures, etc.

2. Then grow!
   Fast growth thanks to a focus on healthy market segments, introduction of new productions, development of new markets, and quality improvements

3. Add capital as you go!
   Implementation of an active capital strategy aimed at gaining external investors who provide the capital for consolidation and growth.

Active recapitalization plays a particularly important role. This is evident in the fact that in two thirds of all successful restructuring cases external capital was added as equity capital and/or outside capital. About three fourths of the crisis companies who were able to implement a capital increase during the crisis

34

achieved long-term positive post-restructuring results. Consequently, capital increase is the most important element of successful financial restructuring. These findings correspond with those of Hotchkiss/Mooradian, who, in their publication "Vulture Investors and the market for control of distressed firms" were able to show as early as 1997 that the pursuit of an active capital strategy delivers the highest value increase potential for prospective investors. In this context, they analyzed the ROI improvements (operational results/balance sheet total) of U.S. reorganization over a period of two years (see Fig. 5).

Those who recognize crisis symptoms too late, or who go so far as to cover them up, lose valuable time, restrict their action radius even further, and squander urgently required resources, such as equity capital or liquidity. Restructuring must then frequently be achieved under time constraints and with little leeway, as well as with minimal resources. Consequently, consultants should approach their work with a focus on implementation. Time for expansive analyses is frequently not available. Mere analyses without instant success in the form of liquidity or earnings improving measures do not do much for a company in an acute crisis. This means that consultants must support the operational implementation of restructuring measures from the very beginning.

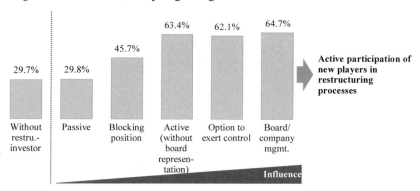

Fig. 5: ROI improvements in U.S. reorganizations over two years [% points]

An acute crisis is always a crisis of trust as well. Unfavorable overall conditions the company cannot control may have worsened the situation, but, as a rule, the majority of all crises are self-inflicted. It takes mismanagement to turn a strategic crisis into an earnings crisis, or even a liquidity crisis. If a company caught in such a scenario approaches banks, credit insurers, suppliers, shareholders, and guarantee providers, such as the federal or state government, for help, a self-critical attitude on the part of executive management is just as indispensable as a willingness to make radical changes. Problems must be openly addressed, and unpopular measures must not be excluded from the approach. If the executives are unwilling to undertake such measures, quick management changes are inevitable. Otherwise the impending restructuring process, which is already under time constraints, would be in jeopardy from the very beginning, condemning all restructuring efforts as untrustworthy and making it impossible to attain consensus.

Every reorganization is complex and unique; there are no patent remedies against corporate crises. Nevertheless after more than ten years of restructuring experience, ten key success factors have been established (see Fig. 6):

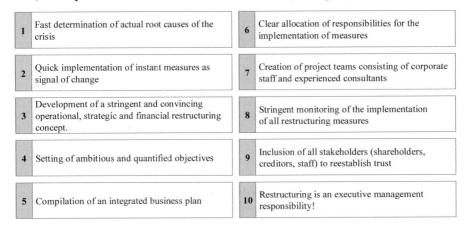

1 Fast determination of actual root causes of the crisis	**6** Clear allocation of responsibilities for the implementation of measures
2 Quick implementation of instant measures as signal of change	**7** Creation of project teams consisting of corporate staff and experienced consultants
3 Development of a stringent and convincing operational, strategic and financial restructuring concept.	**8** Stringent monitoring of the implementation of all restructuring measures
4 Setting of ambitious and quantified objectives	**9** Inclusion of all stakeholders (shareholders, creditors, staff) to reestablish trust
5 Compilation of an integrated business plan	**10** Restructuring is an executive management responsibility!

Fig. 6: Ten success factors for restructuring projects

5 Conclusions and Outlook

Comprehensive and consistent restructuring can play an important role in securing a stable and healthy financial foundation for the company and in ensuring sustainable results and liquidity. It thus clears the way for new strategic options. The effects are positive for all stakeholders; the loan value remains secure for banks and credit insurers, and the related credit rating can be improved. Customers and suppliers will obviously be more interested in continuing their business relations with the company given that they once again consider it a strong and valuable strategic partner. Restructuring offers investors attractive investment opportunities with long-term growth perspectives based on a solid and healthy financial foundation.

Given this background, we are certain that the German restructuring environment will – after the end of "Germany Inc." and the insolvency hype – offer many active approaches that will put companies on a more sustainable long-term footing.

Recapitalization – New Corporate Financing Options

Sascha Haghani, Maik Piehler

1 Financial Reorganization as the Third Restructuring Dimension

Reinhold K., board member of a medium-sized German company, is very enthusiastic about a lucrative opportunity: a profitable foreign partner company has been offered for acquisition at an attractive price. The board member would like to take advantage of this one-time deal to expand his company's business activities. He calls his regular bank to discuss the financing of the acquisition. The phone conversation ends in disappointment: the bank will not provide additional financial resources. Reinhold K. is not alone: right now, many German companies are confronted with similar funding issues – although they have implemented extensive restructuring programs in the past.

In Germany restructuring is perceived very differently from the stance taken in the Anglo-American economy, where the term restructuring is strongly associated with the reorganization of corporate financing. Things are very different in Germany; in this country, the term restructuring to date is linked primarily with improvement of the operational business. This so-called operational restructuring – one could also call it the historical core of restructuring in Germany – thus usually focuses on cost-reduction measures, as well as on optimization of processes and structures. The strategic reorientation, which is closely interwoven with operational restructuring, has been targeting a concentration on profitable core areas and the development of important future markets.

However in recent years, the restructuring approach in Germany has been expanded as well and now also comprises reorganization of corporate financing. The German understanding of restructuring is therefore now three-dimensional: operational, strategic, and financial (see Fig. 1). Consequently, the German approach to restructuring is more comprehensive than the Anglo-American approach, which focuses on the financial dimension.

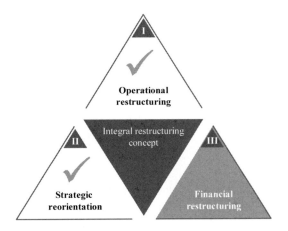

Fig. 1: Three dimensions of restructuring in Germany

This expansion of the restructuring approach can be attributed to two important developments that have changed the patterns of corporate financing in recent years. On one hand, in preparation for Basel II, domestic banks have imposed far more stringent lending restrictions. On the other hand, an ever-greater number of foreign banks and investors have determined that Germany is an attractive market and have developed and expanded their activities in this market accordingly. The increase in potential new providers of funding obviously also affects the existing business relations of German companies with their house banks, which to date have been the primary source for financing.

2 Alternative Financing Options Compete with Conventional Loans

The changes outlined in the previous chapter have opened up new avenues of financing for German enterprises. More and more medium-sized companies are discovering attractive financing alternatives to conventional loans. The bandwidth comprises everything from bonds of all kinds, to a wide variety of mezzanine solutions, to equity capital measures, and in some cases even utilization of the organized capital market. While these tools were available in the past, they were mostly used by large multinational groups of companies. Ever since Anglo-Saxon capital providers entered the market, and thanks to the corresponding responses of the domestic financial industry, access to these types of financing has been facilitated for medium-sized German companies.

For these German businesses this can be a way out of a long-standing dilemma. The restrictive granting of loans by financial institutions, which was further compounded, among other things, by implementation of the Basel II provisions, often hampered required growth investments. Even pre-financing of additional orders is frequently made impossible by the diffidence of credit institutions. By the same token, many medium-sized companies do not have sufficient equity capital to fund growth out of their own resources. However significant earnings advances often cannot be realized without taking advantage of growth options, which would in turn allow the companies to fund themselves. New ways and types of financing can break this vicious cycle.

Over the next few years, financing issues will gain significant importance for medium-sized companies. Especially those going through restructuring will have a continued and increased need for risk-adequate financing. This trend is already clearly evident: in 2005, a growing number of foreign investors acquired loan commitments from German banks. This impacts the entire German financing landscape, in particular the sale of credit portfolios. When new players, whose patterns are difficult to predict, are suddenly involved in existing financial circles and bank pools, this stirs up unrest and dynamics – with the remaining financing banks, as well as the stakeholder companies. This can, to a large part, be attributed to the differences in mentality and corporate culture existing between German house banks with their business bank/savings and loan character on one hand, and the investors with financial investor/investment bank character on the other hand.

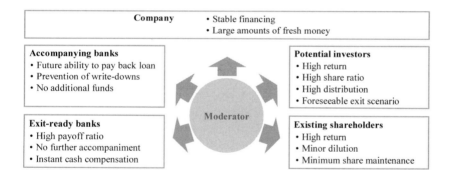

Fig. 2: Moderation and coordination between stakeholders

To this end, all parties involved are slowly getting used to this changed situation. In some individual cases, constructive solutions for applicable corporate financing are already being developed. Overall, however, the affected companies have not yet acquired a full understanding of the objectives and behavior patterns of the new financiers, and of the opportunities offered by the various financial tools. Nevertheless, each individual case requires that the financing solution be adapted to the needs of the respective company. In addition to the standard time and cost aspects (financing terms), this applies to the consideration and incorporation of the interests of the different stakeholders. Their individual interests can differ greatly due to the aforementioned cultural differences as well. The success of such financing/recapitalization solutions thus hinges on the moderation or coordination between the stakeholders (see Fig. 2).

3 A Concept Providing a Foundation for Competitiveness and Growth

Initially, the basic approach to recapitalization is relatively simple: the concept aims at strengthening the financial resolve of medium-sized companies to ensure that they can compete and grow. The stage for long-term market success can thus be set. Normally, integrated recapitalization complements a successful operational reorganization. The concept begins on several levels:

- Provision of new financial resources (fresh money)
- Reduction of the strain on balance sheet and earnings
- Stabilization of the financing circle
- Participation of the financing circle in the success of the company
- Paving the way for strategic cooperation

A heterogeneous financing circle with differing stakeholder objectives is often the starting point for recapitalization. Due to their differing interests, credit institutions have the option to choose between continued financing and withdrawal during the initial stages of the recapitalization process. The logic of recapitalization can be summarized under the following principles:

1. Fresh money prevails over existing commitments
2. Existing financiers have to forsake part of the loan value to withdraw
3. This discount is allocated to the company
4. Institutions that continue to provide financing participate in the company's success

This apparently simplistic logic frequently poses enormous challenges for the companies affected. The differing interests of the parties involved require a lot of moderation and coordination. This coordination of interests and financial tools based on industry experience is one of the key aspects that differentiate recapitalization from purely financially motivated solution approaches.

Depending on the enterprise-specific objective of recapitalization, various tools are integrated. A wholesaler in the southern part of Germany, for example, chose a combination of a capital cut with a subsequent cash capital increase, re-purchase of loans, debt-to-equity swaps, convertible profit participation certificates and variable (result-dependent) interest elements. This allowed a significant reduction of third party liabilities and interest while simultaneously providing funding for additional domestic and international growth. The example clearly showed that improved balance sheet relations – even after a balance sheet cleanup – improve the rating. The now smaller financing circle can participate in the company's future success. The ten months it took to go from a rough concept to technical implementation certainly paid off. The wholesale business was able to strengthen its market position and has returned to profitable growth. Its market capitalization is almost five times what it used to be after just one year – and after deduction of the capital measures it has still doubled.

This project again confirms that implementation of an integrated recapitalization concept usually turns into an exceptionally complex process. This complexity can be attributed to several factors:

- The objectives of the company

- The financing tools potentially available for attainment of these goals

- The differing individual interests of the stakeholders (such as shareholders, new investors, and credit institutions)

- The large number of individual measures/processes and the resulting density of deadlines

- The interdependency between the individual tools, stakeholders and processes

Moreover, when implementing capital measures it is an absolute necessity to comply with a number of regulatory provisions, especially in Germany. To achieve this, specialists such as qualified attorneys, financial auditors, or tax advisors, must be involved in the development of the concept early on. Some agreements that are standard in the United States (such as zero-strike warrants) are not executable in this form in Germany and consequently must be replaced with other tools.

Last, but not least, it is imperative to remember that the demands in relation to internal and external communications of the company increase immensely in connection with a phase of recapitalization. The acceptance of essential, sometimes painful measures by the stakeholders hinges on transparent and convincing communications. Especially companies listed on the stock market must take the interaction with shareholders and specific provisions (for example shareholder options) into account, even in the early stages of the process.

In the recapitalization concept and implementation phases, the elements driving the complexity outlined here translate into a lot of time spent on coordination. Probably the most sensitive task is overcoming the conflicts of interest between the stakeholders. If this is done well, it will go a long way toward a successful recapitalization. This is why the moderator plays a key role throughout the entire process. He or she must be able to transform the trust of everyone involved a solution that can gain consensus.

4 Conclusions and Outlook

Several cases involving the successful recapitalization of companies through innovative concepts attract the attention of other medium-sized companies. We have observed a definitive increase in the interest of these clients in alternatives to conventional loans. Especially after having gone through an operational reorganization, an increasing number of medium-sized businesses in Germany are eager to reinvent their corporate financing. This is just the first wave!

From Crisis to Value Increase: How Companies Can Attain High Profits During a Restructuring Phase

Karsten Lafrenz

1 Crisis Companies Have to Fulfill High Profit Expectations

German corporations are active in a difficult economic landscape. Here are just a few examples of indicators that have a significant impact on Germany's position as a place to do business: Germany's structural unemployment rate is high, which – in combination with declining population growth – puts enormous pressure on social systems and translates into high government spending. On one hand, to fund its expenses, the government has to depend on substantial tax revenues, which in turn means that citizens and corporations must bear a huge tax load. On the other hand, these sizable government expenditures have an adverse effect on investments. Given these factors, in 2004, the economy grew only by approximately 1.5%[1], and the 2005 prognosis does not look any better.

According to a survey compiled by Roland Berger Strategy Consultants, in this economic climate, 42% of the companies interviewed are suffering from crisis symptoms that require management to take corrective action. Successful restructuring hinges on an influx of new capital in most cases, given that once- available equity capital reserves have usually been consumed, or that there is not enough liquidity to fund crisis fighting measures. Another study showed that 65% of the companies who successfully turned things around were able to add new capital.[2] Considering the fact that these companies were in the middle of a comprehensive restructuring phase, an important question arises, namely how can this kind of capital be procured?

In the past, given the standard approach to financing in Germany, virtually all companies in a crisis situation obtained their funding exclusively from their traditional house banks. It is an established fact, however, that the volume of loans extended to businesses has dropped by 6.5% since 2001. It is safe to assume that

---

[1] Ref. German Federal Statistical Office (2005).

[2] Ref. Buschmann (2005), page 180ff.

crisis companies are over-proportionally affected by this trend.[3] The willingness of conventional commercial banks to finance companies in crisis is rapidly declining, especially due to the risk-based capital adequacy rules proposed by Basel II[4], and the pressure on banks to achieve high profits.[5] Consequently, companies are compelled to look for alternative forms and sources of financing. Private equity and hedge funds corporations that are pushing into the German market in droves, and that acquire stakes in the equity and outside capital of the enterprises they do business with, are offering such options. Some key examples: on the equity capital side, KKR invested in Auto-Teile Unger; the Texas Pacific Group invested in Friedrich Grohe. On the outside capital side, Goldman Sachs infused Ihr Platz with funding, while LoneStar invested in Dresdner Bank's non-performing loans portfolio. Anglo-Saxon private equity and hedge funds corporations are also actively involved in restructuring the embattled KarstadtQuelle Group, which made headlines in 2004/2005.

Given the risk position inherent in investing in companies in crisis, financiers bold enough to make new investments in businesses in such precarious situations do however expect a return that few of the affected enterprises can produce, in the form of profits or interest. Corporate loans, which in crisis scenarios must be classified far below the BB rating class, are subject to interest that is significantly higher than 8%; the return expectations of private equity companies in most cases are in excess of 15 to 20% (see Fig. 1). Under these circumstances, companies are increasingly dependent on also generating a return for the investors through a value increase of their enterprise.

For this reason, this article evaluates the options companies in crisis have in their approach to restructuring and what the relevant success factors for restructuring really are (Chapter 2). Based on these findings we then analyze the value increase potential inherent in the restructuring of crisis companies (Chapter 3). Finally, we will look at the impact these findings have on the financing of companies in crisis (Chapter 4).

---

[3]   Deutsche Bundesbank (2005), page 34.

[4]   Second consultation paper issued by the Basel Committee for the Supervision of Banks (2001), or the updated version issued by the Basel Committee for the Supervision of Banks (2003).

[5]   Ref. Eilenberger (2002), page 7ff.

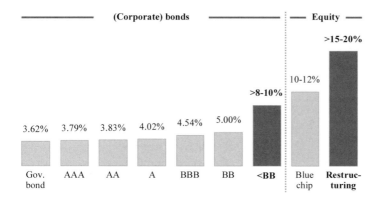

Fig. 1: Comparison of return expectations of investors in Germany [%]
(Source: Datastream, Thompson Financial, Europ. Venture Capital Association)

2 Restructuring Companies in Crisis

2.1 The Four Basic Models of Reorganization

When evaluating the individual approach to, and success factors of restructuring, one must first analyze what models of reorganization are actually available. This is based on the principle that a generally applicable recipe for success, which can be utilized in any crisis, simply does not exist. The author analyzed the restructuring approach of 40 companies listed on the stock market in an extensive evaluation for the period from 1993 to 2002. Roland Berger Strategy Consultants supported all companies as they made their way through crises that jeopardized their very survival.[6] Using a cluster analysis[7] four basic models were identified in the study. Consideration of these four basic types is offered as a compromise between the conflict inherent in making statements, that on one hand are sufficiently specific for individual companies, and on the other hand are also adequate for purposes of generalization The classification of the restructuring models was based on the analysis of the starting point of the restructuring, the measures applied, and the planned process of implementation.

---

[6] For a detailed look at this research, ref. Lafrenz (2004), page 199ff. It should be noted that this number was in some cases further reduced in some analysis steps due to an outlier selection and limited data availability.

[7] For a description of the cluster analysis, ref. e.g. Backaus et al. (2000), page 381ff.

The restructuring approach inherent in these four basic models can be characterized as follows:[8]

- *Efficiency improvement (55% of all companies evaluated)*
  The focal point of restructuring applied by these businesses is on operational
  actions. The dominating factors are cost reductions in production, procurement, and human resources. The strategic orientation remains largely un-
  changed.

- *Refocusing (32% of all companies evaluated)*
  The average companies allocated to this basic model are significantly larger
  than those using the other models and thus enjoy the benefits of a strong
  market position. However, in the course of restructuring, quite few existing
  business segments are given up, and new business segments are developed.
  As a consequence, the overall business focus of these companies changes.

- *Growth (8% of all companies evaluated)*
  Companies using this model are usually rather small. Although they have
  experienced rather strong growth in the past, these businesses have been unable to significantly expand their market share, are cornered in a weak market position, and thus have not reached a critical mass. As they go through
  their restructuring phases they continue to pursue their expansion strategy,
  while trying to implement operational measures to make their growth profitable.

- *Resizing (5% of all companies evaluated)*
  These businesses have also grown significantly in the past. They were, however, unable to achieve adequate profitability levels. The strong revenue decline as associated with restructuring is striking; So that restructuring does
  not only targets cessation of the previous growth strategy, but also results in
  a considerable resizing of the company during the reorganization. One of the
  key measures is reduction of non-core activities, with liquid resources that
  become available being utilized to bring down high levels of indebtedness.

The focus of the next paragraphs will be on the first two basic models, given that
at a combined share of 85%, they cover the majority of reorganization scenarios
and are the most relevant in practice.

2.2 Approaches to and Success Factors of Restructuring Utilizing the Basic Models

Managers of crisis companies will find the following question of critical importance: what does it take to make corporate reorganization successful? To address

---

[8]   These terms differ slightly from those used by Lafrenz, ref. Lafrenz (2004), page 240.

this issue, the key starting points of the described restructuring models are examined below and the respective success factors are highlighted. Given that a restructuring scenario can be allocated to one of the identified models after just a rough analysis, these statements provide important insights into the detailed development of a restructuring concept. The cited survey performed by the author utilized statistically significant differences between those companies that succeeded within a restructuring model, and those that did not, to analyze the key measures and critical success factors. In this context, a successful company is defined as one that achieved significant positive excess returns in the course of restructuring. Companies that produced significant negative excess returns despite restructuring were classified as unsuccessful. Businesses that attained neutral, i.e. neither significantly positive nor negative excess returns were thus excluded from the comparison.

2.2.1 Approaches to and Success Factors of Efficiency Improvement

Efficiency improvement begins with operational restructuring measures. By merely implementing cost reduction measures, they improve return on sales by 8%. Savings are attained primarily in production, procurement, and human resources. Staff reductions by an average of 18% contribute to the human resource cost reduction of 19% (which equals a 5% return on sales). However, significant cost cuts are also possible in the area of miscellaneous operating expenses (on average 12% of such expenses).

Operational measures are accompanied by strategic measures. To improve operational efficiency and effectiveness, the business now concentrates on profitable products, customers and markets. As a result, companies utilizing this model accept an average decline in revenues of 11%. In connection with operational restructuring, the working capital (difference between current assets and short term outside capital) is reduced significantly. By cutting inventories by 15% and receivables by 16%, considerable financial resources can be made available to assist with the funding of the restructuring process.

Another important key to successful restructuring under the efficiency improvement model is the fact that in the past, companies have not optimally utilized opportunities for improvement or streamlining of operational processes, which means that as they begin to reorganize, the level of inefficiency is extreme. This is evident in the fact that the affected companies have considerably poorer productivity indices and also higher production costs than their competitors. A successful reorganization through operational efficiency, however, also hinges on a healthy core business. Whenever the core business can no longer sustain the company's success for the long run, additional strategic measures are necessary. Nevertheless these are much harder to implement in combination with operational problems. Successful companies of this type thus pursue far fewer measures that aim at generating sales through new products or in new markets.

A strong equity capital base is yet another important success factor. The implementation of operational measures aimed at results improvements can burden the results extraordinarily and thus lead to a reduction of equity capital due to special write-offs or severance packages that must be paid. It is therefore of key importance that equity capital availability does not become a limiting factor as restructuring measures are being implemented. If the equity capital does not suffice, appropriate action must be taken to increase it.

An adequate time buffer also plays a critical role in the implementation of the measures. This is of particular importance if new business segments are to be developed while cost reduction measures are being implemented. If the time frame is too narrow, problems will generally occur, given that measures targeting the development of new business segments are usually in conflict with the objectives of cost reduction.

2.2.2 Approaches to and Success Factors of Restructuring

This restructuring model is predominantly characterized by the fact that the affected companies refocus their former business activities in the course of restructuring. To achieve this, existing business segments are given up or sold while new business segments are being developed. As previous business segments are eliminated, revenue levels drop by an average of almost 30%. However, almost half of this decline can be compensated for: the development of new business segments adds an average of 15% in sales.

In refocusing, operational measures are less dominant than they are in the other restructuring models. Cost reductions that yield returns on sales of 8 to 10% in these other scenarios deliver an improvement of only 5% in this model. The key ingredients of cost reduction are a decline in human resource costs (3%) and infrastructure expenditures (1%).

To be in a position to implement the required measures, financing plays an especially critical role in this model. Most of the companies generate the required resources by selling off non-core activities. To provide for adequate liquidity, the existing outside capital is further expanded on one hand, while relatively expansive interest payment deferrals take the pressure off the liquidity of these firms.

One of the key elements of refocusing is a shift in the core business activities of the enterprises. Consequently, corporate flexibility and the know-how applied to the development of new business segments are critical factors for the success of this approach. The size of the company plays an important role as well; as a rule, smaller companies are more successful in utilizing this model than are larger corporations. The former are apparently presumed to be more flexible. Also they generally boast organizational structures that are less rigid, so that they can implement the required changes more swiftly.

Putting the financing on a sound footing is yet another cornerstone for success in implementing the refocusing model; the development of new business segments goes hand in hand with huge financial expenditures. This is true whether such changes are made organically or through acquisitions. Companies that implement this type of restructuring successfully are obviously better equipped to secure funds through the sale of non-core activities than those who do not achieve this kind of success. Successful companies also have less trouble procuring liquidity from outside investors.

3 Increasing Corporate Value Even (and Especially) During the Restructuring Process

As explained earlier, the expected return on investment in the course of a restructuring process cannot be attained merely through interest and disbursements. It must also come in the form of share value increases. The aforementioned survey performed by the author examines the success of restructuring processes based on an analysis of stock earnings.[9] The so-called Event Studies Analysis[10] provides a helpful method to perform this assessment, as it monitors value generation through the progress of stock earnings.[11]

The event evaluated is the launch of a restructuring concept. The examination looks at the effect this event has over a period ranging from 20 stock trading days to two years. The effect of the restructuring concepts was isolated from the general market development through application of the so-called market model.[12] Similar to the Capital Asset Pricing Model it assumes that the anticipated earnings of a security are obtained by weighting the market development with a beta factor and a constant. The difference between anticipated and actual realized return is referred to as excess return. In the survey it is interpreted as the result of the company's restructuring measures.

---

[9] In addition to the mere stock price changes, dividends and other disbursements have been taken into account.

[10] For a description of the Event-Study-Method see Armitage (1995), page 25ff.; Campbell/Lo/MacKinlay (1997), page 149ff.; McWilliams/Siegel (1997), page 626ff.

[11] This article does not intend to discuss the problem of the stock price's deviation from the market value of the company and of an assessment based on the DCF method in more detail. For more on these issues, ref. Süchting (1995), page 396 and Buchner (1994).

[12] Ref. Fama (1976), page 63ff.

When analyzing the success of reorganizations it is evident that positive excess returns, which would create corporate value, were achieved by none of the models examined within a short period of time (less than three months). Positive excess returns are attained in the course of efficiency improvement (plus 1%) and refocusing (plus 98%), only after a time window of at least one year. These increase even more significantly after a longer period up to two years after the launch of the restructuring concept. In the efficiency improvement concept, the excess return jumps to plus 54%, while refocusing produces an increase of plus 136%. For the other two models, due to their minimal representation in the survey, the data available was insufficient to perform long-term evaluations. Fig. 2 shows the development of excess returns.

It must be taken into account that the two models are subject to different risks. While value growth potential is greater in refocusing, an evaluation of the worst 20% of the companies also revealed that this model could result in a total loss (minus 100%). In the efficiency improvement category, the worst 20% achieved a comparably "better" negative excess return of minus 54%.

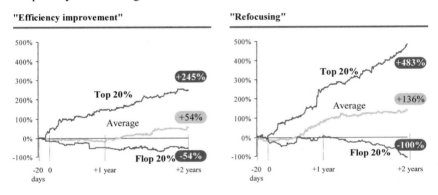

Fig. 2: Cumulative excess returns of identified restructuring models
(Source: in-house calculations)

As earlier indicated, the examined reorganizations were implemented between 1993 and 2002. During this period the stock market produced long-lasting record highs, however, as of March 2000 it was also increasingly bearish. The application of the market model aims at eliminating the impact of the market on the market value of individual companies. Nevertheless it should be noted that the stock market situation does have an impact on the success of restructuring processes. The stock price increases attained by reorganization are far greater during a bullish phase than they are in a bear market. The time it takes to achieve significant increases in equity capital values is also much less in bull markets. In a friendly stock market climate, restructuring activities are not only assessed much more positively than they are in a market of declining stock prices, but investor confidence in the implementation can be generated much more quickly as well.[13]

The analysis therefore reveals that companies are principally able to attain very high returns, and thus extreme increases in their corporate values, over a period of two years. These returns meet or even exceed the high return expectations of private equity funds, so that the latter perceive investments in companies in crisis as attractive options.

4 Summary: Restructuring Yields High Value Increase Potential – Companies Simply Have to Go After It

The survey revealed that restructuring processes offer very high value increase potentials, which are attractive for return-driven investors in Germany also. If companies can convince investors that they can and will realize these value gains, they will be in a position to procure new equity capital as an alternative to conventional bank loans, even in times of crisis. For enterprises battling liquidity problems this type of outside capital sourcing is particularly advantageous, given that their liquidity is not further compromised by interest and repayments.

Analysis of the content of the restructuring models and their respective success factors has shown which measures should be focused on as the restructuring concepts of the models identified are implemented, and which key success factors must be in place. On one hand, recommendations for the layout of restructuring concepts have thus been identified for corporate management stakeholders. On the other hand, the article lists the critical points an investor should verify under any circumstances when performing his or her due diligence for a commitment to a company in crisis. Depending on how much of a risk investors are willing to take, the classifications provided can also be used as selection criteria for the type of investment to be made. Efficiency improvement and refocusing models offer very different return potentials of 54% and 136% respectively, but they are also miles apart in terms of risk profile.

Potential investors of equity or outside capital for companies in crisis are, in particular, specialized private equity financiers of predominantly Anglo-Saxon origin who primarily target companies in crisis – so-called vulture investors. Based on a U.S. study, about 75%, and thus the majority of these investments are made into

---

[13] As a consequence, the percentage of restructuring projects that involve a significant reduction of the company's equity value is significantly higher; ref. Lafrenz (2004), page 283ff.

the outside capital of crisis-ridden corporations.[14] Nevertheless, given that the volume of corporate bonds does play a comparatively minor role in Germany and the transfer of bank loans is not easily possible, it is safe to assume that a far greater percentage of these investments will flow into the equity capital of companies in crisis. Newer loan contracts do, however, allow banks the option to resell their credit commitments. As evident in the case of KarstadtQuelle, this option is actually already being comprehensively utilized. In this instance, private equity corporations acquired tranches of the loan just shortly after a syndicated loan had been granted.

The U.S. study cited above also revealed that the return improvements of crisis companies increases in line with the amount of influence the investors have on the restructuring process. For the respective corporate management stakeholders, however, this means that they will find themselves increasingly confronted with professionally active lobbyists who take advantage of all legal remedies and opportunities, especially on the equity capital side. Few of these equity capital providers have entered the German market to date. Nevertheless, the examples of the replacement of the Chief Executive Officer of the German Stock Exchange, Werner Seifert, or the law suits filed against the squeeze-out of minority shareholders at Wella – albeit not directly crisis-relevant – are first precedents.[15] The possibility of transferring shares between different shareholders confronts corporate management, (but also the other stakeholders, including the loan-providing banks), with a much more volatile composition of stakeholders.

Bibliography

Armitage, Seth (1995): Event Study Methods and Evidence of their Performance. In: Journal of Economic Surveys, Vol. 8 (1995), No. 4, pages 25-52.

Backhaus, Klaus et al. (2000): Multivariate Analysemethoden: Eine anwendungsorientierte Einführung (Multi-Variant Analysis Methods: An Application-Oriented Introduction). 9th Printing, Berlin et al.

Baseler Ausschuss für Bankenaufsicht (2001): Die neue Basler Eigenkapitalvereinbarung: Konsultationspapier, Übersetzung der Deutschen Bundesbank (The new Basel Equity Capital Convention: Consultation Paper, Translation of the Deutsche Bundesbank). In: Basler Ausschuss für Bankenaufsicht (Editors): http://www.bundesbank.de/download/bankenaufsicht/pdf/rules_translation.pdf (Status: 8/1/2005).

---

[14]   Hotchkiss/Mooradian (1997), page 401ff.

[15]   Similar also to Maier (2005).

Baseler Ausschuss für Bankenaufsicht (2003): Die neue Basler Eigenkapitalvereinbarung: Konsultationspapier, Übersetzung der Deutschen Bundesbank (The new Basel Equity Capital Convention: Consultation Paper, Translation of the German Federal Bank). In: Basler Ausschuss für Bankenaufsicht (Editors) http://www.bundesbank.de/download/bankenaufsicht/pdf/CP3_Deutsch.pdf (Status: 8/1/2005).

Buchner, Robert (1994): Zum Shareholder Value-Ansatz (On the Shareholder Value Approach). In: WiSt, Vol. 23 (1994), No. 10, pages 513-516.

Buschmann, Holger (2005): Turnaround Management: Eine empirische Untersuchung mit Schwerpunkt auf den Einfluss der Stakeholder im Turnaround (Turnaround Management: An Empiric Evaluation Focusing on the Impact of Stakeholders in the Turnaround Process), Bamberg.

Campbell, John Y./Lo, Andrew, W./MacKinlay, A. Graig (1997): The Econometrics of Financial Markets. Princeton (NY).

Deutsche Bundesbank (2005): Bankenstatistik: Statistisches Beiheft zum Monatsbericht 1 (Bank Statistics: Statistical Supplement to Monthly Report 1). March 2005.

Eilenberger, Guido (2002): Basel II und seine Entstehung (Basel II and How it Developed). In: Eilenberger, Guido (Editor): Kreditpolitik der Banken und Unternehmens-Rating: Konsequenzen von Basel II: Beiträge zur Konferenz am 28.11.2001 (Bank Loan Policies and Corporate Rating: The Consequences of Basel II: Articles for the Conference on 11/28/2001), pages 7-22, Rostock.

Fama, Eugene F. (1976): Foundations of Finance: Portfolio Decisions and Security Prices, New York.

Hotchkiss, Edith S./Mooradian, Robert M. (1997): Vulture investors and the market for control of distressed firms. In: Journal of Financial Economics, Vol. 43 (1997), pages 401-432.

Lafrenz, Karsten (2004): Shareholder Value-orientierte Sanierung: Ansatzpunkte und Wertsteigerungspotenzial beim Management von Krisenunternehmen (Shareholder Value-Oriented Reorganization: Approach and Value Increase Potential in Corporate Crisis Management), Wiesbaden.

Maier, Angela (2005): Hedge Fonds schaffen einen Präzedenzfall (Hedge Funds Establish a Precedence), Financial Times Deutschland, October 05, 2005.

McWilliams, Abagail/Siegel, Donald (1997): Event Studies in Managerial Research: Theoretical and Empirical Issues. In: Academy of Management Journal, Vol. 40 (1997), No. 3, pages 626-657.

Statistisches Bundesamt (2005): Bruttoinlandsprodukt und Bruttowertschöpfung (Gross Domestic Product and Gross Value Added), http://www.destatis.de/indicators/d/vgr110jd.htm (Status: January 08, 2005), 2005.

Süchting, Joachim (1995): Finanzmanagement: Theorie und Politik der Unternehmensfinanzierung (Financial Management: Theory and Politics of Corporate Financing). 6th Printing, Wiesbaden.

The Financial Restructuring
of Medium-Sized Companies

Robert Simon

1 The Breakdown of Trust Between Banks and Business

"All we need is an expansion of our credit lines, then we will be out of our tempo-rary earnings and liquidity problems in no time." – It is amazing how frequently this very sentence is uttered in the course of negotiations between the executive management of an embattled company and its financial partners. Many executives apparently consider this simple formula a patent remedy in crisis management. However, frequently the required liquidity can no longer be obtained solely on the basis of such an appeal.

Companies usually do not find themselves in the midst of a crisis unexpectedly. Crisis indicators are clearly registered in the proximity of the affected company, especially if the financial partners use sophisticated rating tools. Examples of an impending crisis, which are also felt in the environment of the troubled enterprise, are significant changes in payment transaction patterns (e.g. cash discounts are no longer being taken advantage of), persistently maxed-out credit lines, increased fluctuation in key management functions, loss of expected large orders, failed product innovations, as well as changes in reporting that make it less transparent for outsiders, etc.

Crises in medium-sized companies can typically be attributed to the following root causes:

- There is a lack of succession arrangements, and strife in the family that owns the business

- Control instruments are inadequate

- The company shows weaknesses in management and organization

- Market developments are incorrectly assessed

- Cost structure adaptations are insufficient

- Misguided investments and exorbitant growth result in the excessive capital tie-up

These causes eventually turn into financial weaknesses. Consequently, the mere attempt to get additional liquid funds from financial partners is actually the wrong approach, because it will not suffice. Minimizing the crisis under these circumstances will completely destroy the trust of financial partners and will aggravate the situation. Financial partners expect companies to take substantial measures to eliminate the root causes of crises instead of superficial therapy that addresses only the symptoms.

Within loan-providing banks, credit commitments that are in this kind of jeopardy must be transferred to "intensive care" (for a maximum period of twelve months), or they must be moved from the previous market department to the recapitalization and winding-up department. At the latest when the loan is forwarded to the recapitalization department, the contact persons handling the loan and the objectives of the bank change. Instead of directly providing the required liquidity, the institution now expects the affected company to first come up with a thorough recapitalization concept that ensures the survival of the company and safeguards the bank's commitment, which may be compiled with the assistance of a neutral expert.

Entrepreneurs find themselves confronted with completely new challenges due to this change in support, which hits the company instantly and all at once, together with crisis inherent problems (difficulties with suppliers and customers, upset employees, criticism from other shareholders, etc.) and the looming restrictions imposed on the latitude people in these positions are accustomed to. As a result, they may even react irrationally. In this respect it does make sense to get help from experienced experts.

2   Potential Courses of Action for the Banks Involved

Loan-providing banks generally have two options: termination of the commitment, or approval of a recapitalization loan. These options must be carefully weighed in terms of economic and especially legal aspects, given that they come with a multitude of liability risks (such as termination at the wrong time, quasi-shareholder position, creditor discrimination, insolvency deferral). Fig. 1 shows the spectrum of possible support measures that can be implemented by the banks involved.

	Impending insolvency	Impending excessive indebtedness
Financing of individual transactions	✓	
Deferments	✓	
Conversion	✓	
Deferred installments	✓	
Release of collateral	✓	
Interest waivers	✓	✓
Receivables waivers	✓	✓
Recapitalization loan	✓	
Debt equity swap		✓
Subordination declaration		✓

Fig. 1: Key courses of action available to support companies in crisis from the banks' perspective

If a business customer loan is classified as problematic by the bank and handed over to the internal recapitalization department, a rough analysis of the commitment must be performed as soon as possible (usually within a week). To this end, the feasibility of the commitment's successful restructuring and the realization value of the company's collateral are compared. The client's recapitalization worthiness and ability are also evaluated. If the assessment is negative, the commitment must be transferred to the winding-up department; and the compilation of a recapitalization concept thus becomes superfluous.

If, after performing these preliminary evaluations, the bank is principally willing to remain committed to the crisis loan, it will determine whether all other stakeholders – shareholders and employees of the crisis company, as well as all other creditors – are also willing to support a restructuring process. The reasonable distribution of risks and burdens to all stakeholders is a basic principle. Deviations are only reluctantly accepted.

In the event that the bank arrives at a positive assessment, it will require the crisis company to come up with a recapitalization concept that convincingly shows that sustained industry standard profitability levels, as well as capital service capabilities, can be reestablished through appropriate measures. In principle the enterprise has the option to compile such a recapitalization concept in-house. This actually is common practice with very small commitments that only require the bank to remain patient for a limited period of time. Most corporations are however expected to involve external experts. The reason is a lack of confidence in the skills and critical distance of the management team deemed responsible for the crisis (e.g. unrealistic "hockey stick forecasts"). Moreover, bank and company might find themselves exposed to allegations of intentional creditor discrimination (for example by suppliers) and insolvency deferrals. A credible restructuring attempt hinges upon the presentation of an integral concept developed in collaboration with an expert who is also an industry insider.

Ultimately, these liability issues are certainly a primary reason for involvement of external consultants, but they should not be the only reason. The main goal is to utilize experts with appropriate references who help ensure the survival of the embattled company. In this context, close and trust-based cooperation of all stakeholders is indispensable. Executives or entrepreneurs who view consultants, and the restructuring concept that will be mutually developed, merely as a compulsory exercise, do not meet the standards of recapitalization worthiness.

3 Potential Courses of Action for the Company in Crisis

Until recently, the financing structure of medium-sized companies was usually relatively straightforward. The traditional house bank provided an operational loan (credit line) along with an investment loan with or without institutional subsidies. A few smaller long or short-term commitments of other banks may also have been added. Thanks to new financial tools available, and the increasing internationalization of companies this has changed in some areas. Generally though, when a medium-sized company encounters a liquidity crisis, it usually has financial structures that are still manageable.

Investment leasing, and with some limitations, factoring of revolving receivables, are more recent financial tools that have been accepted by medium-sized business on a grand scale. Factoring competes with operational loans provided by the house bank. If leasing and factoring have not already been used prior to the crisis, they usually do not provide a realistic option to relieve the burden of strained liquidity during an acute crisis. After all, one of the prerequisites for utilization of these financial tools is the long-term reestablishment of creditworthiness.

Due to the dubious prospects of the company, a leasing provider would have good reasons to be concerned about the sale of the leasing product in the event of insolvency – especially if the object in question is hard to sell on. The factoring of mature receivables is a unique approach and also requires that the receivables have not already been collaterized. The factoring organization will also carefully review the future perspectives of the company, given that experience has shown that impending insolvency usually goes hand in hand with deductions from valuable receivables, payment refusals, etc. The potential willingness of the company in crisis to work with potentially risky clients further compounds the problem.

Asset backed securities (ABS) – models that involve securitizing receivables inventories to make them sellable on the capital market – require an adequate volume (minimum commitment currently EUR 5 million) and the company involved must be sufficiently professional. As a rule, ABS models encounter the same restrictions as those discussed in reference to factoring.

Medium-sized companies currently rarely utilize alternative forms of financing sourced from the private equity sector that strengthen the equity capital basis and translate into an influx of liquidity. The struggle of medium-sized enterprises to remain autonomous, which is often emotion-driven, collides with the involvement of third parties who have the capability to influence the process. Alternative approaches that do not affect the ownership structure are certainly available, such as mezzanine capital (for example atypical/silent partnerships, profit-participation certificates, subordinate loans, as well as convertible bonds). As a rule, these long-term oriented offers do however target companies with solid future perspectives. This is the very criterion a company in crisis cannot fulfill – at least not initially. Such options are therefore more likely to be helpful once the restructuring process has been completed successfully.

Risk-oriented funds that come with a willingness to become involved with crisis companies if a positive continuation prognosis has been made, and if the shareholders, as well as the banks, are ready to make appropriate sacrifices, have increasingly established themselves on the German market. In the eyes of entrepreneurs or the proprietor family, this approach is, however, more or less the same as giving up their own business, which is why this option is only considered in cases of extreme emergency.

In summary it must be emphasized that the action radius of companies in the midst of an acute crisis is very limited. The primary focus is placed on cooperation with financial partners who are already committed and thus directly affected, on the remaining potential of the company to fund itself, as well as on possible contributions from shareholders and employees.

In such strained situations, financial partners will be very eager to ensure that individual parties do not receive preferential treatment. Companies in crisis usually find their daily interactions with suppliers becoming more and more complex, given that the latter also play an important financing role through the extension of payment terms. On one hand they are of course interested in continuing business relations; on the other hand they have a great capacity to enforce their interests by stopping shipments and demanding advance payments. Management of working capital and professional communications with all business partners, as well as stakeholders (including credit insurers), are thus of critical importance.

4   The Prerequisites for a Persuasive Restructuring Concept

A restructuring concept must enable all financial partners to determine the concrete measures that must be taken to provide the required support. This translates into a number of requirements in relation to the content of the restructuring concept. It is crucial to disclose the actual economic situation of the company, along with the root causes of the crisis, and to identify and quantify the key levers that will be used to overcome the crisis – all with the objective of making a statement on the recapitalization capability and worthiness of the enterprise. The business plan, upon which the concept is based, must cover a period of at least three years, it must be conservative, and it must reflect the critical risks. It is therefore common practice to principally discuss the concept in advance with the house bank and the other banks that have the greatest exposure.

It is the responsibility of the consultants to ensure transparency, in particular in relation to the entire financing structure, earnings and liquidity development, as well as the restructuring risks. While this is to be done in collaboration with the company, consultants must maintain a critical distance. It could very well be the case that the consultant concludes that the company is not in a position, or is not worthy to be recapitalized. Given that consultants take on liability toward banks and other creditors if they make incorrect or incomplete statements, and due to the fact that their own image might be tarnished, consultancy work must always be performed retaining a professional level of distance and autonomy. The latter is ultimately the deciding factor for the credibility of the restructuring concept. This imposes exacting demands on the skills of the consultant and his or her communications with key decision makers in the crisis company, since medium-sized companies are typically fixated on just a few individuals in leadership positions.

In this regard the personality of the entrepreneur might be both a company's strong point, and its weakest point simultaneously. It is he or she who drives the company, and who surrounds himself or herself with other executives that fit his or her style and implement his or her or ideas. This could very well be the root cause of the enterprise's adaptation problems when market conditions change and the dominating entrepreneur does not recognize this fact in a timely manner. In these person-oriented structures potential successors are in jeopardy of failure. Consequently, the entrepreneur and the corporate executives play a key role in the restructuring process.

In addition to the classic approaches aimed at cost reduction and the identification of future market opportunities, a positive continuation prognosis for the business also hinges on the outcome of the management skills assessment. The restructuring concept must show that the implementation is ensured through measures plans that identify the responsible individuals, milestones, and the material effects of the individual measures. The management team's and shareholders' written commitment to these measures, as well as a transparent project organization with appropriate reporting are absolutely essential. Otherwise there is imminent danger that the restructuring will not be implemented in a target-oriented manner once the required resources have been provided.

Financial partners consider the fact that all financial contributions from the remaining stakeholders must be bindingly listed as a further minimum requirement of a persuasive restructuring concept. Some examples:

- Shareholders: equity capital replacing loans, capital increases, withdrawal waivers, refund of withdrawals

- Executives/staff: relinquishment of portions of their wages and salaries for limited periods of time, deferral of special bonuses (recapitalization wage contracts, etc.)

- Company: reduction of working capital, stringent expense reduction, sale of non-operating assets, foregoing of added comforts

- Suppliers: deferral of due dates on receivables, solidarity contribution

Given the enormous time constraints under which restructuring concepts are usually drawn up (in particular in cases where the insolvency application period has been initiated), this is an amazing challenge that can sometimes only be met to a lesser degree. However, some agreements with shareholders and employees can only be made if the threat of insolvency is looming. These are good reasons why the financial partners are hesitant to compromise.

This article does not address the legal and tax-relevant aspects. They should however already have been taken into account in the concept phase. If failure to do so necessitates changes to the concept at a later date, then this can undermine the trust in the capabilities of the crisis managers. It is certainly extremely helpful and recommended to discuss these and other issues in advance with the legal department of the lead bank.

5 Agreements with Financial Partners

The company will have a good chance of coming to an agreement with its financial partners if the key stakeholders attest that the restructuring concept has a high likelihood of succeeding, and if they do not want to lose the company as a future customer. This is ultimately the rational formula of success that must be considered by the executive management and/or the entrepreneur.

In preparation for the negotiations, the restructuring concept must be presented to the financial partners, and transparency in terms of the banking and collateral scenario must be provided. If the business is family-owned and operated, the interface between company and private life must also be disclosed (rental agreements, withdrawals, guarantees, etc.).

Typical, but not always required is establishment of a collateral pool by the financial partners, if they can come to an agreement with the company as far as a continuation concept is concerned. Formerly this was a given, but this is no longer the case. The traditional concept, which caused banks and, possibly credit insurers, to form a cooperative of interests based on the principles of equal allocation of the burdens and risks, is no longer applied as extensively as it was in the past.

This is partially due to the fiercer competition between banks that have to protect their own earnings situation. Due to the individual allocation of collateral, as a rule, not all financial partners are equally affected by the insolvency of the company, which can limit the level of solidarity the partners are willing to extend. This is particularly true if a bank, due to the modified business focus of the underperforming commitment, no longer considers it as part of its core business. Contrary to the basic principle, this constellation allows direct replacement of troublesome financial partners. Achieving debt moratoriums with these partners would already be considered a success.

From the bank's point of view, the impact of the crisis engagement on the bank's own refinancing is yet another deciding factor. Banks are also subject to rating, and their ratings are adversely affected by a high level of exposure to default risks. In lieu of the time-consuming and risky restructuring, sale of the problem loan with respective discounts to a specialized fund is therefore a rational option. Of course this is at odds with the above principle, but currently it is simply a given fact. In a joint engagement aiming at saving the company in crisis, the financially strong and crisis-scenario-specialized fund will of course pursue its own interests. This may very well be the fast turnover of its title on improved terms or – alternatively – obtaining an opportunity to buy additional key shares of the credit portfolio by replacing additional financial partners at even lower prices. This portfolio may eventually be exchanged for actual stakes (debt equity swap).

These processes happen outside of the direct sphere of influence of the affected company in crisis. Without substantial financial resources of its own – which have been consumed in most cases – entrepreneurs and shareholders are left with just the one opportunity to make their earnest restructuring concept credible as they strive for continuation and a means of financing the business.

In some cases, entrepreneurs also attempt to replace financial partners by submitting a joint offer with a new partner along with the expectation that the departing partner will waive entitlements. This strategy does, however, go hand in hand with high risks for the overall success of the negotiations: those financial partners who are strongly engaged will ask themselves why the funds are suddenly being made available now that the situation has reached a crucial stage, and why they are not being utilized directly for restructuring. Banks who are ready to get out can take a different stance on this. In the event of any discrimination, the acute meltdown of the agreement process looms due to principal considerations.

It is, on the other hand, not unusual that financial partners view the entrepreneur or the shareholder structure as a key cause of the crisis and are therefore convinced that the sale of the company in crisis to an investor at the earliest possible date is a necessary restructuring measure. In such a case concessions in favor of the investors are an option. The forming of trusts is a common step taken in preparation of this measure.

The parameters for a final agreement with financial partners are highlighted in Fig. 1. Based on current experience, the feasible results are debt moratoriums, as well as interest and principle deferrals to take the pressure off of the company's liquidity. In the meantime, fresh money must be regarded as an exceptional achievement. Direct receivables waivers of financial partners in favor of the company are only negotiable if the equity capital is in extreme jeopardy, and they are more likely to occur after completion of a long-term restructuring process, during which radical measures have been implemented. As a supplementary note it should be mentioned that these supporting measures are subject to risk surcharges, which must be taken into account when planning capital services in the future.

Given that the financial partners expect additional collateral (such as guarantees, pledges) for their patience and possible additional financial contributions, no free collateral will remain once the agreement has been finalized. Financial measures or changes to the financial structure at a later date, such as factoring or asset-backed securities, are possible only in coordination with the financial partners, who will expect at least some payments on loans out of the resource influx.

Once the agreement has been made, the company's ultimate goal must be to implement the strategic and operational restructuring process with enthusiasm and success so that lost credibility is reestablished. This requires regular communication to that end. If this (final) restructuring attempt fails, there usually will not be a second chance.

Changes in Due Diligence Requirements

Nils von Kuhlwein

1 Due Diligence in a Time of Change

Due diligence, which refers to the systematic verification of the truth and fairness, as well as the diligence of a company's management in relation to risks and potential, have long become part of every corporate acquisition – although infamous exceptions to this rule do indeed occur time and again. Transactions sealed with a handshake, which used to be a tradition in Germany, usually end with the buyer discovering some very unpleasant surprises, which, in not so infrequent worst case scenarios can translate into writing off the entire investment. What follows are lawsuits in court, and lengthy, tedious disputes with both parties fighting over the legitimacy of the purchase price paid. The costs of such proceedings frequently far exceed the investment one would have to make in due diligence prior to the acquisition. Another important argument for due diligence is the fact that in an increasingly complex, globalized economy, the impact of a corporate acquisition and the strategic and financial policies of the business that will potentially be acquired is not transparent for an investor without comprehensive and detailed analyses; even if the buyer is an industry insider. A diligent and comprehensive verification of the truth and fairness of the target company's management is therefore an absolute prerequisite in ensuring the transparency needed to make a purchasing decision. Moreover, due diligence is the key source of information based on which buyer and seller will negotiate the type and amount of potential guarantees and warranties for the respective acquisition object.

2 Types of Due Diligence

As a matter of principle, one distinguishes between the different types of due diligence based on who actually performs the process: if it is initiated by the prospective buyer of an investment object or company, the investigation is referred to as buyer due diligence. If the seller takes the initiative, the process is called vendor due diligence. Historically, buyer due diligence was the first to be performed. Originally, the audit was performed by the buyer or by a specialist contracted by the former, in order to obtain the necessary transparency for a purchase decision. In recent years it has, however, become an increasingly common practice that the seller performs a vendor due diligence for the object of sale, to establish the required transparency prior to the intended sale. Based on the information obtained, decisions are made concerning the handling of potential selling process risks, the time needed, and the optimum timing for respective measures and steps to be taken in the sales process.

Apart from the buyer or vendor classification, due diligence can also be differentiated by audit and evaluation areas. The following are typical classifications:

- *Financial due diligence:* audits the historical, current and planned asset, financial, and earnings situation of the company,

- *Strategic due diligence:* evaluates the strategic positioning of the purchase object, its strategic development potential, the market and competitive scenario, as well as possible synergies inherent in the merger with the acquiring company,

- *Technological due diligence*: assesses the technological position of the purchase object, in particular in terms of future investment requirements and, if applicable, existing investment bottlenecks from the past; it also includes a partial due diligence of the IT environment,

- *Legal due diligence*: a legal investigation into the status of the company, in particular an investigation of important contracts,

- *Environmental due diligence*: the assessment of potential environmental risks,

- *Employee due diligence*: an evaluation of human resources related risks; in particular the legal review of contracts (such as employment contracts, site security agreements), company agreements and if applicable, existing social plans,

- *Tax due diligence*: the assessment of the potential tax risks inherent in the purchase object, as well as possible transaction and financing structures,

- *Management audit*: verification of the qualification of the existing management (top level and tier 1).

As a rule, the buyer utilizes external specialists to investigate the individual audit areas. One of the benefits of this approach is that external, neutral third parties will not be suspected of making their performance of the due diligence a platform to spy out business secrets. Moreover, most buyers do not have the necessary staff resources to come up with the required specialized know-how. Given that different specialists are frequently used for different audit jobs – attorneys, financial auditors, and consultants – established and clearly defined classifications have developed (e.g. legal due diligence and financial due diligence).

For the most part, due diligence work has the characteristics of an audit. To determine the truth and fairness of management in the respective sub-segments, an audit that is based on random check and individual case verification must be performed. This applies in particular to financial, legal, environmental, employee and technological as well as tax due diligence. Consequently, due diligence processes place a lot of focus on past events: by analyzing past business events they attempt to identify purchase price relevant risks for the buyer. These risks may already exist latently or may establish themselves in the future. Most components of strategic due diligence as well as verifications of forecasts performed in connection with financial due diligence are exempt from this strong focus on the past.

2.1 Buyer Due Diligence

Buyer due diligence is an audit performed by or on behalf of the buyer or prospective buyer of a company. As a rule, this kind of due diligence is executed in a predefined data room. The seller provides such a data room and stipulates how long this room will be open to be used by several potential buyers (one after the other or, if multiple copies of data room records are available, also simultaneously), or for how long it is available for a single prospective buyer only. After the data room has been closed, usually after a period of two to three weeks, the prospective buyers are invited to submit a purchase offer for the business. The data room generally provides access to documents and information that allow the prospective buyer to perform an adequate audit of the truth and fairness of the purchase object management. If additional questions arise, they are collected by the seller or his agent. In the end there is a decision regarding whether, to what extent, and in what form responses will be provided to these questions.

More recently utilization of so-called electronic data rooms has been increasing. In this case, all documents are scanned and stored in an electronic register, which is accessible to individual employees and consultants of the respective prospective buyers via the Internet with the assistance of specially assigned passwords. The process allows buyer-specific preparation of documents to protect confidential information; appropriate shadow numbers can be assigned, certain information can be blacked out. This approach is particularly practical if several interested parties intend to perform a complex due diligence in a minimum amount of time. While utilization of an electronic data room is more complex for the seller, as the due diligence phase progresses it shortens the overall duration and reduces the level of seller consulting required. In practical applications, an electronic data room yields the following benefits:

- The electronic data room can be kept open 24/7.

- The approach translates into less travel time for buyer teams, given that the electronic data room can be accessed worldwide. This is particularly important for multinationals, where due diligence involves innumerable documents in different languages and complex special topics (e.g. environment, taxes).

- Major due diligence projects, which frequently involve more than one hundred consultants, the mere number of participants frequently results in a logistics nightmare in terms of accommodations and handling. For instance if several bidders desire to perform a buyer due diligence, the company would have to verify each data room copy, which often consists of hundreds of file folders, for completeness.

In everyday practice, standardized data room indices have been established for management of data rooms. As a rule, they contain information on the following subjects:

A. General company information; trade register excerpts, charter, important partnership agreements

B. Finances; in particular annual reports, corporate earnings statements and profit contribution statements, as well as respective commentary

C. Management/staff information; contracts, company agreements, evaluations, analyses, and organization charts

D. Management information systems; minutes of committee meetings, and IT infrastructures

E. Sales, marketing, market, and competition

F. Products and product development

G. Strategic planning

H. Legal aspects

I. Research and development

J. Tax aspects

K. Miscellaneous, such as quality indices and manuals

2.2 Vendor Due Diligence

In recent years it has become quite common for sellers to perform their own due diligence. These vendor due diligence projects usually begin before the sales process is initiated and are often used in place of buyer due diligence. The results of the vendor due diligence, which has been performed by a neutral external expert, are made available to interested buyers, who do not receive direct access to a data room. This method is frequently utilized by groups that are selling subsidiaries for the purpose of keeping the intent to sell hidden from the purchase object management team as long as possible, or to prevent unnecessary unrest at the sales object provoked by a large number of external visitors to the data room. Prospective buyers are merely permitted to ask the seller selected questions based on the vendor due diligence records. In some cases a limited data room may also be made available to the potential buyers. It is common practice to make an additional data room available to a limited circle at a later time, for instance if the parties have basically arrived at an agreement on the possible purchase price (so-called confirmatory due diligence). This room then contains fundamental records and contractors or documents in which the portions that had been blacked out during the vendor due diligence have now been made legible.

Vendor due diligence, gives the seller more control over the procedure and accelerates the auditing process, similar to utilization of an electronic data room. This is particularly advantageous if the sale is handled through a bidding or limited auction process. Vendor due diligence enables the seller to keep the auditing expenditures manageable for prospective buyers until a well-founded declaration of intent has been issued, which means that a larger number of potential investors can be kept in the race longer. Large and complex sales objects, in particular, are virtually impossible to expediently investigate for external prospective buyers who are not intimately familiar with the company, or the task is simply too time-consuming to tackle. In particular financial investors, who in preparation of a transaction, aim at keeping the auditing costs to an absolute minimum, would be driven away by time-intensive and cost-intensive investigations, especially if due to the bidding competition they cannot be certain that they will actually close the deal. Vendor due diligence also facilitates provision of differing information to a variety of buyer groups; for instance by blacking out sensitive data in information submitted to key competitors, while making it legible for financial investors.

In addition to maintaining control of the process, as described above, sellers find vendor due diligence particularly helpful in unearthing purchase price reducing risk prior to the planned transaction. This provides the seller with a solid basis for determination of the sales price; unpleasant surprises during price negotiations or seller exclusion criteria are prevented accordingly. After all, as a rule, risks can then be discussed and clarified before sales negotiations actually begin, or they can be openly circumscribed in the course of price determination. On the contrary, if critical risks are not discovered until a buyer due diligence is performed; then the potential danger that prospective buyers will become so unsettled that they will not make an offer, is huge. An increase in trust that develops in the course of due diligence is one of the prerequisites of a successful selling process. If the seller damages or destroys this trust by not openly communicating risks, the buyer will usually look for high security discounts in relevant purchase price considerations.

However, vendor due diligence can also uncover the need for corrective action to render the business sellable. This is particularly true if crucial gaps in the records that will later be made available in the data room are discovered in the course of such due diligence. Early detection of this defect provides the seller with plenty of time to close these gaps prior to initiating the sales process. If such gaps, for example insufficient documentation of forecast calculations, were unearthed during the performance of a buyer due diligence, this would have a negative impact on the negotiations, such as a delay in the transaction process, buyer misgivings, and as a result, a potential reduction of the purchase price offered.

Last, but not least, vendor due diligence ensures that the potential buyer is provided with a consistent set of financial data, and other data. In this context it is imperative that the information contained in the sales memorandum, the management presentation, as well as in the completion of supplemental questionnaires – during and after the due diligence, and until the contract is signed – provides a uniform and harmonious picture. Inconsistencies will result in time-consuming queries, clarification efforts, and misgivings that frequently also result in a reduction of the purchase price.

3 Special Requirements During Restructuring and Insolvency

Due diligence plays a special role in restructuring and insolvency processes, given that in an insolvency a verification of the truth and fairness of management is no longer relevant, and in a phase of restructuring the decision as to whether the company actually has a future frequently is more heavily weighted than investigations of mistakes that have already been made. In both cases, the focus of due diligence must therefore be placed on an assessment of future perspectives rather than on an investigation of the past. Moreover, in case of restructuring it is highly likely that a restructuring concept has already been developed. Companies that are insolvent will generally already be in possession of an insolvency plan, or a concept for a hive-off vehicle. Under these circumstances it makes sense to place the emphasis of an audit on validation of the existing concepts. As a rule, the general valuation criteria

- Essentiality
- Correctness
- Transparency
- Completeness and
- Clarity

Should be applied and weighed against each other. From the prospective buyer's viewpoint, the correctness and completeness of such concepts will be the most important criteria, since they ultimately determine whether the concept is feasible and the purchase price is justified. In restructuring cases, verification for completeness and correctness encompasses the standard scope of restructuring concepts that have been established from the experience gained by performing a large number of projects.

This includes:

- The description of the company
- The analysis of the current economic scenario and the root causes of the crisis
- The vision of the restructured company, in particular the derivation of the results improvement objective
- The measures to attain the vision and
- A thorough, detailed and integrated business plan

The first step in the audit process is therefore determination of whether and to what extent the standard scope was complied with. The second important audit step focuses on establishing whether the vision of the restructured company can be stringently derived from the situation assessment, and whether the measures to be taken to attain the vision are transparent for outsiders, whether they are gleaned strictly from the analysis of the situation, and whether they have the potential to sustainably eliminate the root causes of the crisis. In a third audit step the extent to which the measures have been mapped out in the business plan is then verified:

- Have the measures been incorporated completely?
- Can the business plan be derived from the measures?
- Will the objective be sustainably attained through the business plan?
- Are the other assumptions in the plan plausible?

The audit tasks in the insolvency environment are largely similar to those common during restructuring processes. The main focus here is also on concept plausibility, albeit with a unique difference: at least as far as the operational portion is concerned, the concepts are usually not derived through an analysis of the scenario. Consequently, a highly important plausibility component is obviously missing, given that the vision and the measures to attain it are based primarily on the analysis of the situation. Moreover, for legal reasons, the seller will not provide any guarantees for sales out of insolvency. The buyer will thus have to consider all potential risks when coming up with a purchase price offer.

4 New Trends in the Due Diligence Process

Almost every single corporate acquisition involves the performance of due diligence. Originally this meant that balance sheets were reviewed, the entrepreneurial and financial situation of the business was analyzed, and all legal and tax relevant risks were assessed. However, the due diligence process has become increasingly complex. Just a decade ago, due diligence in a sizeable company took just a few weeks and required a small number of internal and external experts. Today a multitude of different consultants is frequently required to analyze the various aspects of the purchase object. The large number of failed takeovers in recent years has also led to an even more complicated process for buyers. After all, this has further increased the desire for more investment security in strategic, as well as financial, investors. More and more potential buyers, in particular financial investors are now relying on consultants who manage the entire due diligence process on their behalf. These consultants are held responsible for ensuring that everything goes according to plan, but they also perform the actual due diligence. In other words, they ascertain that everyone involved in the due diligence knows what to do and when to do it. To solve this complicated task professionally, consultants utilize project-monitoring tools, which can also be applied to complex implementation projects. Such tools provide consultants with a consistent overview of the status of their due diligence, for example through application of a simple "traffic light system". Whenever deviations are discovered as the project progresses, appropriate measures can be taken with the assistance of these tools.

Another trend developed in the financial investments segment, which particularly affects distressed debt investments and quasi-auction sales. In these cases the success of a financial investor hinges primarily on the former's ability to get a favorable purchase price and his capability to correctly assess future opportunities and risks. An even more critical, deciding factor, however, is often the potential value gain achieved by the time the investment is resold. Prior to making a purchasing decision, financial investors thus require a certain level of clarity in relation to the expected value increase, and the interest of potential buyers after the maintenance and value increase period. The scope of a traditional due diligence process does not adequately achieve this. If a company is traveling through calm waters and maneuvering in a stable competitive environment, it is possible to predict future performance improvements to a certain degree, based on the current business position, market, and competitive scenario. This tends to be far more complicated – if not impossible – if the company is caught in the midst of a crisis.

It has therefore become increasingly common to evaluate the added value opportunities of such companies early in the due diligence process. In this context, a preliminary, rough schedule for turnaround of the company in trouble is developed – usually with the assistance of a top-down approach. This method has proven to be efficient and practical. It is frequently sufficient to verify whether management's actions to date have been diligent and vigilant. This, supported by external benchmarks, allows certain conclusions to be drawn in relation to the root causes of the crisis. As a rule, the most important measures that will bring the company back on track can be derived from the results of such an investigation. This approach usually ends with a 100-day plan, which allows the financial investor to attain a corporate turnaround in the shortest possible time – with the help of corporate management, and if necessary, with an external consultant. Such 100-day plans generally include the following aspects:

- Definition of a specific improvement goal based on a target return (ROS or ROCE); the improvement goal is usually derived from the benchmark values of competitors with the strongest performance
- Derivation of specific attainable potential, focusing on this potential
- Rough definition of first steps to be taken to attain the potential
- Development of a work program that defines the objectives and steps for the first months of the investment in detail

As soon as the investor has acquired the company, the 100-day plan can be used to define the new direction the company is to take. Consequently, the investor does not lose any valuable time after the acquisition. He or she can completely focus on important issues from the beginning, i.e. on increasing the value of the investment through profit and liquidity boosting measures. Speed is ultimately the most critical success factor in corporate reorganization. Consequently, financial due diligence in a restructuring/insolvency context is much more future-oriented than conventional due diligence.

Part 2: The Results of the Latest Surveys Performed by Roland Berger Strategy Consultants

German-European Restructuring Survey 2004/05 – Results and Recommended Courses of Action

Max Falckenberg, Ivo-Kai Kuhnt

Every insight is an identification of the different
Friedrich Wilhelm Nietzsche

1 Survey Results

In keeping with this quote from Nietzsche, we have expanded our established restructuring survey from 2001 and 2003 beyond the German borders to Europe. In the second half of 2004 and in the first months of 2005, Roland Berger Strategy Consultants performed a comprehensive study of the root causes and success factors of restructuring projects in Europe. In the course of the survey the consulting firm interviewed about 2,600 management board members and directors, representing companies from various industries. About 700 German businesses were in this mix. Both the 2001 and the 2003 German studies were used as the basis for the current European restructuring survey. The evaluation comprised businesses that implemented a restructuring project in the past three years. To this end, we placed special emphasis on compiling and providing comparisons between the Western European, Central and Eastern European (CEE) countries.

The results of this German-European restructuring survey will be presented on the following pages. In this context, we are applying the same structure we used during the survey: it was divided into seven blocks of topics, and we asked each of our interview partners for their respective assessments:

- The time of crisis intervention

- The success factors of restructuring

- The elements of restructuring

- The importance of human resource measures

- The importance of early warning systems

- Special resource needs for restructuring

- Restructuring as a permanent responsibility

1.1 Early Crisis Intervention

1.1.1 Germany

Our survey clearly indicated that German businesses have learned to react more swiftly when they find themselves in a crisis. A time comparison shows that since 2001 the reaction speed of companies has accelerated. A respectable 32% of the companies interviewed responded as soon as they recognized a strategic crisis (2001: 20%). However, 51% (2001: almost 57%) will take action only when symptoms of a results/earnings crisis appear. Another 17% (2001: 23%) wait until they have actually entered a liquidity crisis before they take countermeasures.

Typically, a course of crisis begins with the strategic crisis. In a strategic crisis, a company will, among other things, continue to focus on shrinking markets, underestimate new competitors, keep core products that have long surpassed the zenith of the product life cycle, and ignore changes in customer behavior patterns. Failure to implement measures counteracting the crisis, sooner or later results in progression to the results/earnings crisis, and depending on the liquidity reserves available and negative cash flow, soon advances to a liquidity crisis. As the crisis process unfolds the company action radius becomes smaller and smaller. The pressure to take action increases considerably and reaches its peak in the liquidity crisis.

Early and speedy countermeasures principally yield better restructuring results. Our experience, accrued in more than 1,500 restructuring projects confirms as well that timely and consistent responses to crises lead to the greatest success. The companies interviewed agree: should they ever need to go through another restructuring process, they would take respective measures faster and with greater consequence while applying large objectives focus (28%) and would begin their restructuring efforts sooner (23%).

1.1.2 Europe Without Germany

The evaluation indicated that CEE companies in particular tend to react much later to a crisis than Western European businesses. A total of 29% of all Western European and CEE enterprises reacted already during a strategic crisis. The major difference between the crisis reactions is evident in the results/earnings crisis. Most of the Western European firms (62%) react at the latest when they miss profit and profitability targets, i.e. when they enter the earnings crisis. One of the key factors is the increased pressure imposed by stakeholders. In CEE, a results/earnings crisis motivates only 46% of the companies interviewed to initiate turnaround measures. The high number of businesses who do not recognize the seriousness of their situation until they are stuck in a liquidity crisis (26%) is troublesome indeed. In particular Croatia and Romania cry out for improvement and in Western Europe only 9% of the companies wait that long. The fact that early warning systems have only been sparsely implemented in CEE countries, which is one of the main reasons for the delayed response, will be discussed separately.

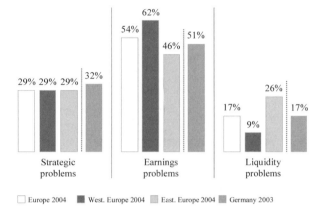

Fig. 1: Reactions to crisis symptoms
(Source: Roland Berger Strategy Consultants, Restructuring Survey 2005)

The comparison of crisis reaction times clearly shows the faster responses to crises in Western Europe. While 54% of all interviewed Western European companies had already initiated a restructuring process within the first twelve months, this is true only for 49% in CEE (Germany 2003: 64%). The difference is even more striking in a comparison with time frames of 12 to 24 months: another 42% responded during this period in Western Europe, in CEE only 32%. This means that an amazing one fifth of all the companies included in the CEE survey reacted only after two years; a waste of valuable time.

On average, European firms react more slowly than German companies. When comparing our German 2003 survey with the European 2004/2005 results, German companies, who attained an average crisis reaction time of 14 months, outperform the European average of 16 months.

Our project experience and this survey evidence that it is a fast response time, in particular, that aids the success of a project: 74% of those interviewed were satisfied with their project success if the measures were initiated within twelve months following the appearance of symptoms.

1.2   Restructuring Success Factors

1.2.1   Germany

The executives interviewed indicated that management commitment is one of the central elements of success, along with fast implementation and the integral approach of the restructuring concept. However, it also became apparent, that there is indeed room for improvement, especially in terms of implementation. To this end, only 35% of the companies interviewed were very satisfied with their managements' commitment and a mere 33% were satisfied with the implementation speed. Our project experience also confirms that the commitment of management is one of the key factors for restructuring success.

1.2.2   Europe Without Germany

What we had already learned from the German survey in 2003 is equally true for Europe: management commitment is considered to be the most important restructuring success factor, and was cited as the number one guarantor for success by 67% of the Western European companies. In Eastern Europe, a respectable 55% agree with this assessment. Implementation success is considered a problem in Europe as well: while it achieves better marks in Eastern Europe (40%) than in Germany (36%), the results are still very moderate.

The top 5 Western European success factors correspond with those listed in the German survey:

1.   Management commitment

2.   Fast implementation

3.   Integrated concept

4.   Intensive project monitoring

5.   Close cooperation with the workers' council

The success factors in CEE reveal a different picture: approaches such as creative problem solutions and shareholder engagement make the cut instead of cooperation with the workers' council and project monitoring. Implementation of best-practice methods, for example, was considered a key success factor only in a few CEE countries.

Strategic reorientation was brought up as a critical restructuring success factor only occasionally, except for Poland: where strategic reorientation is the number 2 priority. As a rule, the companies interviewed see an integrated concept (rank 3) as an important success factor and presume that it includes a strategic reorientation.

In terms of all of success factors considered highly important, companies do fault the level of implementation. As we had learned earlier in Germany, inadequate implementation was also considered a problem in Europe. Ergo: the necessary steps were identified, but they are not being consistently implemented (see Fig. 2).

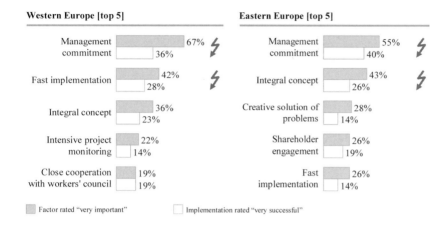

Fig 2: Restructuring success factors Western Europe vs. CEE [% of companies – multiple answers possible]
(Source: Roland Berger Strategy Consultants, Restructuring Survey 2005)

1.3   Restructuring Elements

1.3.1   Germany

Understanding of restructuring processes has expanded: for quite some time it has not referred solely to planning and implementation of cost cutting measures. Companies are betting increasingly on revenue boosting activities. To this end, 82% of the companies interviewed (in 2001 it was a mere 49%) also implemented sales-up programs in conjunction with their restructuring programs.

1.3.2   Europe Without Germany

Staff reductions and human resource expense cuts play a primary role with the Western European executives we interviewed. More than 90% cited these measures as components of their restructuring concept. At close to 90%, material cost reductions were the third most frequently listed cost cutting measure. In Western Europe, as in Germany, the focus is therefore clearly on lowering costs.

While cost reductions also play an important role in CEE, revenue-increasing programs were considered to be the most important measure in these markets

(90%). So-called sales-up programs are also a key ingredient in the other countries (after cost reductions). In CEE, the general objective is to produce almost 44% of the earnings increase through increased revenues. At 48%, this expectation is even higher in Western Europe, albeit only 30% in Germany.

1.4   The Focus on Human Resource Measures

1.4.1   Germany

The survey did confirm that staff reduction is considered a key operational restructuring measure. In addition to conventional workforce reduction tools (termination agreements, natural fluctuation, part time agreements with older staff members, operational terminations), consensus-oriented and innovative solutions are increasingly being utilized during reorganizations. This includes compensation waivers (employee contribution), outplacement companies, and reorganization wage agreements. In Germany, however, the termination agreement absolutely continues to be the most frequently utilized staff reduction tool. The desire to keep matters harmonious (consensus) is still largely intact.

The survey also clearly indicated that cooperation with the workers' council could considerably increase the overall success of a restructuring project. This is yet another example of the dominance of consensus-oriented staff reductions.

1.4.2   Europe Without Germany

In Europe, on the other hand, the scene is still being dominated by conventional tools: the focus, at the rate of 60% is on operational termination, followed by part time agreements with older staff members (58%), and reductions through natural fluctuation (57%). At 30%, salary and wage reductions play a subordinate role. The relatively high percentage of reorganization wage agreements in CEE, where this method ranks fifth at 38%, is notable also.

1.5   Utilization of Early Warning Systems

1.5.1   Germany

Companies consider utilization of tools for early detection of crisis symptoms to be crucial. This includes, for example, management information systems (MIS), a rolling liquidity outlook, regular review meetings, risk management systems, and increasingly the application of balanced scorecard models.

It has however also been determined that such control and early warning systems have so far been inadequately implemented. For instance, only 57% of the companies interviewed actually possess a monthly management information system, although 96% emphasize the importance of this tool for early crisis detection (see Fig. 3).

Tools	Europe		CEE		Western Europe		D 2003	
Monthly management information system (MIS)	77%	65%	74%	43%	80%	84% !	96%	57% ⚡
Monthly review meetings with corporate divisions involved	75%	60%	72%	43%	77%	75% !	80%	46% ⚡
Rolling liquidity forecast	53%	44%	53%	31%	52%	56% !	71%	54%
Key performance indicators/ balanced scorecard	50%	30%	41%	17% ⚡	58%	42%	63%	27% ⚡
Risk management	44%	24%	48%	21% ⚡	41%	27%	67%	35%

☐ Very important   ☐ Fully implemented

Fig. 3: Early warning systems for crisis detection [% of companies]
(Source: Roland Berger Strategy Consultants, restructuring survey 2005)

Especially companies with revenues between EUR 100 and 500 million either lack the tools to detect crises early on completely, or they are not utilizing them adequately. Overall, only 38% of these businesses possess a completely implemented management information system, and only 17% have a balanced scorecard model in place.

Companies with completely implemented early warning systems were in a position to undercut the average response time (14 months). Requiring an average of nine months: companies who had balanced scorecards in place were the quickest to react.

1.5.2   Europe Without Germany

In Europe, early warning systems are not assigned the same level of overall importance that they enjoy in Germany. The result: the average reaction time is close to 16 months compared to Germany's 14 months (see Fig. 4).

84

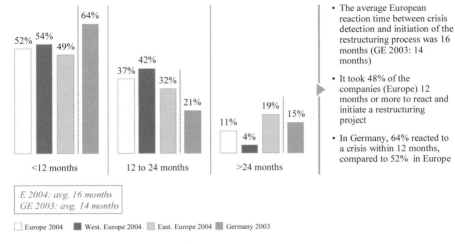

Fig. 4: Crisis response times in relation to high tool implementation levels
(Source: Roland Berger Strategy Consultants, Restructuring Survey 2005)

By comparison, 77% of all participants interviewed consider management information systems (MIS) a crucial tool. A respectable 65% have even implemented an MIS. It was however not possible to determine from the survey that utilization of MIS as a tool reduces crisis reaction times.

On the other hand, only 50% of the companies rate the balanced scorecard as an important tool, although in Europe too those companies that have implemented balanced scorecards are the quickest to react (eleven months) in the event of crises (the average company takes 16 months). The good news is that the implementation level is also slightly higher at 30%.

So-called review meetings are widely used all over Europe (60%) and considered important (75%), although they frequently fail to deliver the anticipated effect and only reduce reaction times to twelve months.

Another striking observation is the fact that of those companies caught in an acute liquidity crisis; only 30% have implemented a rolling liquidity forecast. This means that the majority of companies in crisis remain virtually blind in terms of their future development, even when they are already in trouble. Lack of liquidity forecasts is one of the key reasons why a large number of businesses will react only after they are in an apparent liquidity crisis.

1.6   Special Restructuring Resources

1.6.1   Germany

A need for special restructuring resources was indicated by 80% of the German companies surveyed. The funds are primarily provided (80%) through intra-group financing. Bank loans rank a distant second (37%). Other financing options (e.g. capital increase, capital market financing, factoring, sale and leaseback) were utilized by only 10 to 20% of the companies reviewed.

1.6.2   Europe Without Germany

The overall situation in Western Europe is similar to that in Germany. More than 70% of the businesses are in need of additional resources. In Central and Eastern Europe, less than 60% report such a need. At 59%, intra-group financing plays the most important role in the sourcing of funds in Europe as well (see Fig. 5).

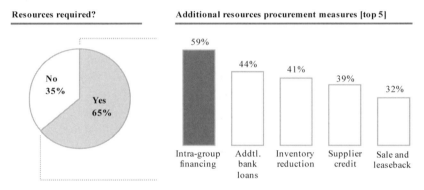

Fig. 5: Additional resource needs for restructuring and measures to procure them (Source: Roland Berger Strategy Consultants, restructuring survey 2005)

Just like in Germany, bank loans take rank two at 44%. Ranks 3 through 5 go to working capital measures and sale and leaseback. Capital market financing and shareholder loans are not included among the Top 5. In the medium-term, it is however safe to expect things to change, as is evident in Germany right now, given that the funding sources that are currently being utilized are limited, and the role of banks has begun to change radically throughout Europe. The changes caused by the provisions of Basel II and the currently still high risk positions at banks will further complicate the granting of outside capital financing by the banks. Alternative forms of financing, such as mezzanine capital will be utilized more extensively in the future. The increasing acquisition of companies by private equity companies, such as Blackstone, CVC and Permira, will also translate into new financing options.

1.7 Restructuring as a Permanent Responsibility

1.7.1 Germany

Only a small percentage (20%) of the companies had already finalized their restructuring process at the time of the survey, or saw a low probability for additional restructuring measures in the next two years. At the vast majority of the firms, restructuring continued (52%), and 42% consider restructuring to be a continuous process.

Deciding factors behind this skeptical attitude, according to the majority of the companies surveyed, are the continued weak economy (54%), and declining prices (38%). The scarcity of bank loans motivates only 11% of the companies to implement additional restructuring measures.

In our opinion, the minimal economic growth in Germany, which is primarily the result of low domestic demand and increased cost pressure as a result of EU enlargement, as well as global competition, will require further restructuring in the future.

1.7.2 Europe Without Germany

An understanding of restructuring as a continuous process is far more prevalent in Europe than it is in Germany (63%). Moreover, the process is still in its early stages. Not even 10% of the companies claimed to have already completed their restructuring process, and another 30% explicitly stated that their reorganization was not yet finalized.

The presumption that additional measures will be necessary stems in particular from the increased competitive pressure (35%) and the weak economy, which is also being felt in Europe (27%). Other factors, such as globalization, new technologies, or industry reactions, were rarely mentioned (less than 20%).

2 Summary Survey Results and Recommended Courses of Action

Germany has made progress in almost all categories of our survey and is now Number 1 in Europe in terms of response speed to crisis symptoms. This is evidence of a continued tough economic climate in Germany, which has significantly accelerated the response times.

In addition to essential cost reduction measures, German companies are placing more and more emphasis on revenue boosting programs. The importance of growth strategies in the aftermath of revenue consolidation is therefore being taken into account.

In the CEE countries improvement potential in the area of early warning systems certainly exists. Respective action should be taken in terms of liquidity management, in particular.

While the survey results for Western Europe and Germany are similar in a lot of areas, Central and Eastern Europe appears to be a clearly younger restructuring region. Due to a lack of experience, crises are detected later than anywhere else, and restructuring measures are implemented slower than anywhere else. The high emphasis on revenue boosting programs and their share in the improvement of overall results evidence the region's belief in the market. The second focal point, material costs, suggests that this is the first time these companies actually have to tackle a restructuring process.

In summary, we have determined that corporate restructuring has been further institutionalized and that many companies consider it a permanent responsibility for good reasons. The successes of concepts implemented enhance the competitive edge of businesses sustainably, even though concept sustainability must be closely monitored through early crisis detection and warning systems.

The most frequently cited weakness is long-term concept implementation, which concurs with our project experience. We consider implementation one of the key action items.

Based on the survey results and time sequence comparisons the following are the recommended courses of action:

- It is important to react quickly to a potential crisis

- Early crisis detection tools must be utilized effectively

- A detailed concept must be implemented consistently

- Clear management commitment is an absolutely essential prerequisite for restructuring success

- The early incorporation of all stakeholders in the measures increases the implementation speed and the success

- A mere focus on cost reductions will not suffice. Long-term success hinges on revenue-boosting measures

Distressed Debt in Germany from the Banks' Point of View

Nils von Kuhlwein, Michael Richthammer

1 Introduction

Given that the German economy had to cope with close to 40,000 corporate insolvencies in 2004, the number is very likely to hover around this high level in 2005 as well. Along with the increasing number of insolvent corporations and companies who are no longer able to meet their liabilities to credit institutions, the number of loans seriously at risk of turning into losses, so-called distressed debt, is rising rapidly.

Since the mid-90s the extensive sale of these types of loans has gained a very high level of importance in the Anglo-Saxon markets. In the meantime, this issue is also making waves in Germany and has most certainly stirred up the banking industry. One of the most talked-about cases is the IRU (Institutional Restructuring Unit), a division of Dresdner Bank, which has sold approximately EUR 25 billion in "dubious loans" since 2002. Another is HVB Real Estate that sold a credit portfolio value at EUR 3.6 billion to U.S. investment firm Lone Star. Some banks were also observed opting for the sale of their loans to withdraw from their engagement in the KarstadtQuelle restructuring scenario. All of these cases are indicators that German banks have now also discovered this exit option and that they are increasingly taking advantage of it.

To obtain a more in-depth view of the German distressed debt market, Roland Berger Strategy Consultants performed a comprehensive survey under the title "Distressed debt in Germany from the banks' point of view" in 2005. In conjunction with the study, questionnaires were sent to about 60 German banks. To obtain a representative profile of the German banking landscape, the survey addressed banks from different segments and of different sizes. The objective of the inquiry was to record the assessment of the market and the future development of the German distressed debt market from the banks' point of view. To meet this objective, here are some of the questions the banks were asked to respond to in connection with the survey:

- When did banks begin to look into the distressed debt scenario and why?

- What are their market activities?

- How large is the market volume and how will it develop in the future?

- What are the overall conditions that impact the German distressed debt market?

- What experiences have the market players had?

2 Key Findings of the Survey

In this section, the key terms will initially be defined to ensure uniform understanding. Subsequently, the most important results of the survey will be presented. To this end, we are following the structure of the questionnaire, which was divided into the following topics:

- General information on distressed debt

- Current status of the distressed debt market in Germany

- Overall conditions of the distressed debt market in Germany

- Operational execution and the transaction costs

2.1 Key Terms

To arrive at a uniform understanding of the terms used in this article, we will explain the different *distressed debt types* and *transaction forms*.

In reference to *distressed debt types,* the survey follows the usual division into loans and bonds. The different loan categories are business loans, consumer loans and mortgages/real estate loans.

Transaction type debts are categorized as *single-name*, *basket* and *portfolio* transactions. Whenever a title in a distressed debt type loan is acquired, it is called a *single-name* transaction. If several titles in a distressed debt type loan are acquired, the transaction is referred to as a *basket* transaction. Last, but not least, a *portfolio* transaction involves the purchase of several titles of various distressed types.

2.2 General Information on Distressed Debt

In the first part of our general information on distressed debt survey, we asked banks how long they had been engaged in the distressed debt business and to tell us why they are dealing with distressed debt. We also inquired into their opinion on the root causes that result in loans being classified as distressed debt. The banks were also asked to explain which warning systems they trust, which role they themselves play in the market (seller, buyer or both) and what types of distressed debt they are engaged in, or in what form they trade it. They were also asked to answer questions on their transaction volume, transaction frequency and any discounts given in connection with such transactions.

One of the first key results of the survey is that 86% of all survey participants are engaged in distressed debt. A respectable 38% of respondents indicated that they had been operating in this area for more than five years. This shows that even in Germany a large percentage of banks has been actively utilizing this market for many years. The improvement of their own risk assessment/structure or the objectives of credit structure improvement were cited as the primary reasons for distressed commitments. The banks' own creditworthiness or rating, as well as the return on equity play only a subordinate role.

Of the survey participants, 67% claimed that they approach the market as sellers only. This definitely emphasizes the fact that banks are first and foremost keen to adjust their loan portfolios. The remaining 33% act as sellers as well as buyers; which allows the conclusion that these banks, in addition to adjusting their loan portfolios, are also intent on making a profit through the active trading of loans and that they are actively engaged in buying loans to expand their own position. Not a single German bank acts as a mere buyer, however, only very few banks do so worldwide.

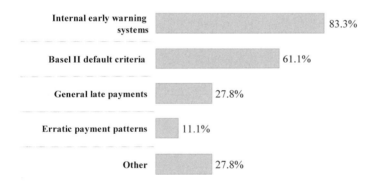

Fig. 1: Prerequisites for the classification of loans as distressed debt [% of survey participants, multiple answers possible]

In classifying loans as distressed debt, banks rely primarily on their in-house early warning systems. In addition, they utilized default criteria pursuant to Basel II in order to classify loans accordingly. General default on payment or irregular payment patterns are of subordinate importance from the banks' point of view. This indicates that banks place more trust in their in-house warning systems, and do not rely exclusively on the obvious criteria, such as late payments or inconsistent payment patterns. The majority of banks actually do have proven early warning systems in place that reliably alert them to loans in jeopardy (see Fig. 1).

Survey participants cite liquidity crises and declined sales as the prime reasons for distressed debt. They also blame equity capital risks and uncompetitive cost bases for the trouble corporations find themselves in. Efforts to secure ratings or having to post earnings below the return objective, on the other hand, are not viewed as causes of distressed debt (see Fig. 2). In summary, these points clearly show that a company must be in an advanced state of crisis with characteristics that lead to insolvency, such as a liquidity crisis, or equity capital being in jeopardy, before loans are classified as distressed debt.

Fig. 2: The causes of distressed debt based on the experience of banks [% of survey participants, multiple answers possible]

When asked which distressed debt types they are engaged in, 94% of the banks questioned listed business loans, with mortgages/real estate loans coming in a close second at 89% (multiple answers were possible). Only half of the banks deal with distressed debt in consumer loans, and only 39% have such engagements in bonds. This information indicates that the focus of distressed debt is primarily on large volume loans, given that business loans or mortgages/real estate loans usually involve much greater amounts than consumer loans. This is also evident in the information provided by banks on the nominal volume of distressed debt transactions. In both business loans, as well as mortgages/real estate loans, more than 70% of all transactions hover above the EUR 100 million mark. Transactions involving a volume of less than EUR 50 million are indeed the exception in the distressed debt business (see Fig. 3).

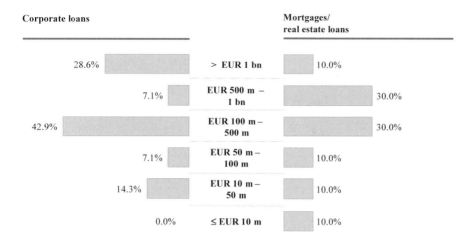

Corporate loans   **Mortgages/ real estate loans**

Corporate loans		Mortgages/ real estate loans
28.6%	> EUR 1 bn	10.0%
7.1%	EUR 500 m – 1 bn	30.0%
42.9%	EUR 100 m – 500 m	30.0%
7.1%	EUR 50 m – 100 m	10.0%
14.3%	EUR 10 m – 50 m	10.0%
0.0%	≤ EUR 10 m	10.0%

Fig. 3: Nominal volume of distressed debt transactions of the banks surveyed 2003/04 [%]

An evaluation of transaction frequency clearly shows that only very few banks perform regular distressed transactions, i.e. several times a week or month. A total of 72% of the banks claim to perform such transactions only if they come up. In other words: they leave the process up to chance and do not actively initiate such transactions. They engage in distressed debt business only when the opportunity arises. This attitude is prevalent with those who are merely interested in selling and shows that they do not actively offer their "bad loans" to the market, but that they simply react to a demand that has consistently increased in recent years. We will therefore have to wait and see whether this rather passive attitude on the part German banks will turn into a more active and market driving approach in the years to come.

The inquiry into discounts given during a transaction (on the nominal value) also produced interesting results. The surveyed banks claimed that discounts of less than 10%, or in excess of 50%, on the nominal value are not granted. In 25% of all cases, the discounts are somewhere between 10 and 20%, in 8.3% of the transactions, 20 to 30% is given. This means that discounts are between 30 and 50% in almost 70% of all cases, with reductions by 40 to 50% cited most frequently. They make up 41.7% of all transactions. This means that in most of these transactions, 50 to 60 cents are paid for each euro in nominal value. At this time, we can, however, not conclude with absolute certainty whether these price concessions are the result of the actual market price of the loan, or whether they are also the result of other discounts (e.g. if the bank wants to sell the loan as quickly as possible).

The evaluation of the distressed debt portion of banks' total loan volumes revealed that it is in excess of 10% with 7.1% of the banks surveyed, while 85.7% claimed that distressed debt makes up less than 7.5% of their volume. A respectable 35.7%

of the banks cite a share below 2.5%. Other sources support these figures, estimating the distressed debt portion to be an average of about 5% of the total credit portfolio of German banks. Based on this information it is safe to assume that the figures we came up with during our survey are correct and representative.

2.3   The Current Status of the Distressed Debt Market in Germany

How do banks rate the status quo on the German distressed debt market? To get answers to this important question, we queried banks on their assessment of the current market volume, the expected changes in market volume, as well as the transaction volume they expect to see in the next few years.

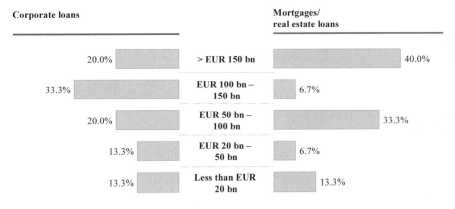

Corporate loans

Mortgages/ real estate loans

Fig. 4: Estimated nominal value of distressed debt in Germany 2005

The distressed debt market volume in Germany is estimated to total approximately EUR 300 billion. If one considers the most frequently cited business loan and mortgage/real estate loan values reported by banks in our survey, this assessment can be confirmed. Most banks claimed that the total value of business loans classified as distressed debt is somewhere between EUR 100 and 150 billion, with most estimating mortgages/real estate loans at more than EUR 150 billion. This would coincide with the frequently used estimate of EUR 300 billion. The allocation in Fig. 4 does however indicate that survey participants arrive at very different estimates in relation to market volume.

Most of the surveyed banks expect the distressed debt volume to rise, while they are looking for stronger growth in 2005 and 2006 than in 2007. Fig. 5 backs up this prognosis. The growth predictions do differ significantly nonetheless. As evident in relation to the assessment of the market volume, it is true here as well that German banks have not yet arrived at a homogenous understanding of the distressed debt market, and that their market volume/growth estimates are thus worlds apart.

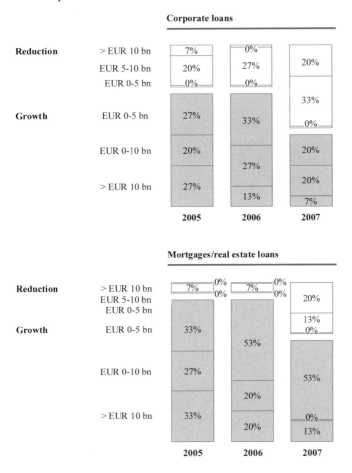

Fig. 5: Development of the distressed debt volume in Germany

While the assessment of the distressed debt transaction volume points toward a slight increase in business loans, the surveyed banks expect mortgages/real estate loans to see a decline in this area. Business loan transaction volume projections for 2005 hover around the EUR 13 billion mark. For 2006 figures are expected to increase to approximately EUR 15 and 14 billion respectively. In other words, the transaction volume will presumably further increase in the years to come. Consequently, business loan trading will remain an important issue. For 2005, banks forecast mortgage transaction volumes to reach EUR 16 billion. For 2006 and 2007, on the other hand, projections call for this figure to drop to EUR 14 and 10 billion respectively. Ultimately, the volume of business loan transactions would therefore exceed the volume of mortgages/real estate loans, and as a result, would dominate the market.

The projected development of transaction types is interesting. In 2005, making up more than 50% of the total volume, portfolio transactions clearly dominate the picture. Their share however is expected to drop to less than 42% by 2007. At the same time, the percentage of single-name transactions will accordingly jump to 30% (from 27% in 2005), while basket transactions will make an even bigger leap from 21% in 2005, to 27% by 2007. The surveyed banks are thus anticipating that more targeted and more individualized transactions – primarily single names – will squeeze the formerly dominant loan packages (portfolios) out of the market. This, on the other hand, would invite the conclusion that German banks have completed their gross loan portfolio adjustments, and that the adjustments will be more targeted in the future.

2.4   Overall Conditions in the German Distressed Debt Market

In this section we will look at banks' assessment of the overall conditions in the German distressed debt market. Banks were asked to comment on the impact banking secrecy and data protection provisions have on active loans and what the potential solutions would be. Banks were also questioned about the potential adverse impact German insolvency statutes might have on the German distressed debt market (in comparison to the United States).

First, banks were asked to list the problems that could occur with transactions of active loans due to banking secrecy and data protection. In response 69% of the banks confirmed that because of these issues only non-performing loans and loans with express debtor approval are being offered. Only 13% reject this causal cohesion. The question as to whether the problem loan client contact will remain with the seller produced rather diverse responses. Of the surveyed banks, 44% view this as an obstacle, while 31% do not agree with this statement at all. The query as to whether legal uncertainty compounds the risk that transactions are revoked drew similarly mixed input. A slight majority of 44% felt this was the case, while 38% checked the "do not agree" box.

Subsequently, various options that could provide starting points to solve the problem were highlighted and the banks were asked to comment. The results are shown in Fig. 6.

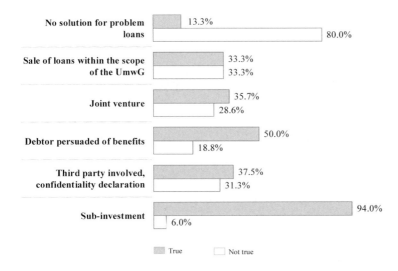

Fig. 6: Options for addressing problems in relation to banking secrecy/data protection[1]

Survey participants felt that bank secrecy/data protection related problems could best be solved by attaining sub-stakes in the loan. This eliminates respective buyer conflicts, i.e. given that buyers are now co-owners of the loan, they are permitted to review confidential documents. Banking secrecy would consequently not be breached. A respectable 50% of the banks are also under the impression that it would be helpful to convince the debtor of the advantages inherent in selling the loan. An impressive 80% of the participating banks indicated that there are, in principle, ways and methods to bypass the banking secrecy/data protection issue. In other words, banks do not view banking secrecy/data protection as a risk that could cause a transaction to fail and that could adversely affect the attractiveness of the German distressed debt market for prospective investors.

In addition to banking secrecy and data protection, German insolvency statutes could also have an impact on distressed debt investing in Germany. The fact that German law differs greatly from corresponding U.S. legislation could have a particularly negative effect on the attractiveness of the market. German banks do however take a wide variety of stances on this issue: 38% opine that the different insolvency statute philosophy (survival in the United States versus creditor protection in Germany) could drive investors away. On the other hand, 44% feel that this does not hold true. There is a wide consensus that the flexibilities inherent in

---

[1]   Only categories "true" and "not true" are shown, category "don't know" has not been included.

the German insolvency statutes are not being taken advantage of to their full extent, and that this is definitely detrimental: 56% of the banks surveyed agree with this perspective, only 25% reject it. The structure of German insolvency statutes is principally viewed to have some negative impact: 44% of the banks are of the opinion that the insolvency statutes do have persuasive characteristics and do not offer the same options that are provided by U.S. law.

In addition to the insolvency statutes, Germany does have a number of other legal provisions that can affect distressed debt investing. A total of 69% of the banks surveyed felt that collateral pools do have a major impact on distressed debt investment patterns. Collateral pool agreements frequently prevent banks from withdrawing from loan arrangements prematurely. As a result, many loans are not even offered for sale, which limits the options available to potential investors. Half of the banks surveyed feel that special loans, which are frequently being granted in Germany, such as the KfW loan, do have an adverse effect on the market, given that they cannot be sold. Consortium loans influence investment patterns according to 44% of the banks. Respective contracts prohibit banks from withdrawing from the loan consortium. Many banks that consider the sale of a loan are being prevented from doing so due to these regulations. This exit channel is simply not available to them. As a consequence, the potentially existing market volume is kept low by statutory provisions.

On the contrary, banks do not view the German protection against dismissal law, which makes it difficult to terminate staff, and which frequently hampers restructuring efforts, as an influential factor. This law, which has recently been criticized because of disadvantageous regulations for employers, does not have an adverse impact on the attractiveness of the German distressed debt market from the banks' point of view. The IFRS accounting principles are also not considered detrimental for the German market.

A total of 86% of the banks surveyed responded positively to the question of whether they see long-term problems for investors operating without a banking license. Only 19% feel that this will not cause any problems. Banks cite the following reasons that necessitate banking licenses:

- A banking license is required to buy active loan commitments

- A banking license is a prerequisite for fresh money in recapitalization cases

- Without a banking license, an investor does not have the option to enter into balance settlement agreements (cash collateral, guarantees)

Banks also see a potential risk for the illegal and non-registrable utilization of creditor positions.

We will have to wait and see whether problems actually do develop. It is, however, noteworthy that some Anglo-Saxon distressed debt investors are increasingly trying to obtain stakes in German credit institutions. The participation of

JC Flowers & Co. and of Shinsei Bank, Japan, in the NordLB and WestLB joint venture is one such example. Investors are obviously trying to get around the problem of not having a banking license by going that route. This was at least the reason why U.S. financial investment firm Lone Star took over the Mitteleuropäische Handelsbank (MHB) from NordLB, or why Cerberus secured a banking license at the end of 2004 when they acquired Sauerland-based HKB-Bank.

2.5 Operational Execution and Transaction Costs

In this section of the survey banks were asked to assess the experience of market players, as well as transaction experiences, and the difficulties incurred. They were also invited to comment on the exit strategies they would consider suitable.

From the banks' point of view, distressed debt investors are considered to be the most experienced market players: 83% of the banks surveyed evaluate their own level of experience mostly with low grades. Only 22% rated their experience as "high". The majority of the banks admit that if they have a deficit in experience compared to investors who frequently have an Anglo-Saxon economic background.

Law firms and business consultants are viewed as highly experienced market players by 44% or 28% of the banks surveyed. This means that the banks rate the level of experience of these consultants higher than their own, albeit much lower than that of investors.

In summary, this means that from the banks' point of view none of the other market players in Germany is currently on a par with specialized distressed debt investors. Neither the banks themselves, nor attorneys or business consultants, have a similarly comprehensive level of experience. In the next few years they will consequently have to go through a learning curve before they will be considered as full-fledged market players.

With the information provided by the banks surveyed in response to the request to assess the experience and difficulties with transactions it becomes evident that banks have little experience with business loan transactions and that they rate the level of difficulty inherent in such transactions as "high". Only 39% of the surveyed banks give their experience with business loans high marks, while 28% classify their level of experience as low. The picture is completely different with bonds, where 80% of the banks surveyed cite high levels of experience and 73% do not see any difficulties with bond transactions. The results are almost the same for mortgages/real estate loans, where 67% claim high experience levels and only 39% see any difficulties. In other words, banks do indeed have experiences with bonds as well as mortgages/real estate loans, while based on their own feedback, the majority of German banks still lack this know-how in relation to business loan transactions.

100

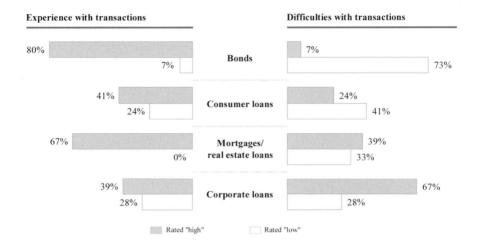

Fig. 7: Experience and difficulties with transactions[2]

In response to questions concerning their experience in selling loans, 65% of the banks surveyed cited comprehensive experience. A total of 59% claimed that they did not have any experience with the sale of guarantee/letter of credit sales. The responses to queries concerning the level of difficulty confirms these results: 63% of the banks rate the level of difficulty for guarantee/letter of credit sales as "high", while only 29% feel this way about loans. This would indicate that they trade in loans far more frequently than they do in guarantee/letters of credit.

Responses to questions about the key cost blocks of transactions provide an interesting insight (see Fig. 8). The primary cost estimates of seller and buyer are miles apart in this area: according to sellers, information and data processing costs produce the highest cost block – 33.8% of overall costs. Attorneys' fees and contract development form another key cost item at 23.4%. Consequently, at the seller's end, more than 50% of the total costs go toward information and data processing, as well as legal fees. This indicates that sellers place a lot of emphasis on obtaining information/analyses (53.3% of the total expenses) and on the drawing up of the agreement, and that they commit the majority of their financial resources to these expenses.

On the buyer side, the picture looks totally different. While legal expenses/contract drafting makes up the total cost block at 18.3%, review of information and assessment are estimated to consume only 14.4% and 15.5%. A total of 33.9% of the overall costs is spent on the exit, while 12.9% is utilized for cor-

---

[2]   Only categories "high" and "low" are shown, category "average" has not been included.

porate restructuring. The allocation shows that the exit plays a major role in the eyes of the buyer and that consequently a majority of the financial resources is dedicated to this necessity. From the banks' point of view, the restructuring of the company is one of the key exit strategies and is therefore frequently given preference over other strategies, such as sale or liquidation.

Sellers' viewpoint

Information procurement/ analysis ∑ 53.3%	33.8%	Information/ data processing
	11.8%	Assessment/ target price
	7.5%	Contacting investors
Handling ∑ 44.7%	14.3%	Provide/service data rooms
	23.4%	Legal advice Contract drafting
	7.5%	Transfer charge
Other	1.8%	

Buyers' viewpoint

Information procurement/ analysis ∑ 39.4%	14.4%	Information review
	15.6%	Assessment
	9.4%	Third party info procurement
Handling ∑ 24.4%	18.3%	Legal advice Contract drafting
	6.1%	Transfer charge
Exit ∑ 33.9%	7.2%	Sale to third parties
	12.8%	Restructuring
	13.9%	Other exit options
Other	2.2%	

Fig. 8: Percentage of key cost blocks in the total cost of a transaction[3]

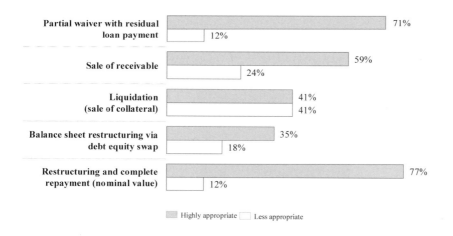

Partial waiver with residual loan payment	71% / 12%
Sale of receivable	59% / 24%
Liquidation (sale of collateral)	41% / 41%
Balance sheet restructuring via debt equity swap	35% / 18%
Restructuring and complete repayment (nominal value)	77% / 12%

 Highly appropriate ☐ Less appropriate

Fig. 9: Appropriateness of exit strategies[4]

---

3   Average.

The response to the last question of the survey confirms that from the banks' point of view, corporate restructuring and the complete repayment of the loan are the preferred exit strategies: 77% of the respondents felt this approach was "highly appropriate", only 12 rated it as "less appropriate". However, 71% of the banks also view a partial waiver with residual loan repayment as a potential strategy for ending the loan arrangement. A respectable 49% of all banks still consider a resale of receivables "highly" appropriate, while liquidation and the subsequent sale of respective collateral gets much lower marks from the banks. While 41% of the respondents considered this solution suitable, an equal number rated it as unsuitable (see Fig. 9).

As a matter of principle the banks' primary interest is in restructuring the company and getting back their entire loan volume. Other options that require the bank to give up a part of the customer payments are always considered to be a secondary option.

3   Conclusions and Outlook

This section provides a brief overview of the most important survey results. For a graphic overview, please refer to Fig. 10.

First and foremost, most banks view their own experience in this area as very limited, although they have been active in the distressed debt market for years. Especially in comparison to distressed debt investors, the vast majority of German banks claim to have a huge experience deficit. In the next few years the focus will necessarily be placed on eliminating this deficit.

The study also shows that banks tend to operate their distressed debt transactions rather opportunistically. It remains to be seen whether they will leave their relatively passive position in the years to come, and whether they will become more active in the market. Furthermore, banks live with significant discounts ranging from 30 to 50% of the nominal volume. However, it is still unclear whether these discounts are caused exclusively by the actual market price of the loans sold, or by additional rebates granted by the banks.

The survey delivered yet another important result: traditional restructuring and the satisfaction of nominal value remain highly preferred exit strategies. As a matter of principle, banks are first and foremost interested in restructuring the affected

---

[4] Only categories "highly appropriate" and "less appropriate" are shown, category "somewhat appropriate" is not included.

company and in ensuring that loans are paid off in full. Other options, which require banks to give up part of the debtor's payments, are always considered to be the second-best solution.

1. Most banks rate themselves as inexperienced although they have been selling distressed debt for years

2. Banks (currently) are in this business for opportunistic reasons and are willing to live with substantial discounts

3. Nonetheless, conventional restructuring and repayment of the nominal volume are highly preferred as a solution

4. The corporate loan and mortgage distressed debt markets both exceed a nominal value of EUR 100 bn

5. In the next few years, the transaction volume will increase significantly and level off at approx. EUR 15 bn

6. The market will clearly move away from portfolios and will favor single-name transactions

7. Investors will not be able to do this kind of business in Germany without banking licenses

Fig. 10: The key findings of the survey

In reference to market volume estimates, the distressed debt market for business loans and mortgages/real estate loans totals in excess of EUR 100 billion in each case. There are, however, vast gaps between the figures submitted by the banks surveyed, which indicates that the banks do not yet have a homogenous picture of the German distressed debt market.

The information provided by the banks also points toward a future market volume of about EUR 15 billion per annum for both the business loan and the mortgage/real estate loan transaction volume. In 2007, the volume of business loan transactions is expected to exceed that of mortgage/real estate loan transactions.

In reference to transaction types, the market will clearly move away from portfolio transactions and toward single-name transactions. This is an indication that German banks have completed their rough credit portfolio adjustments and that future adjustments will be more targeted.

It should also be taken into consideration that 80% of the banks surveyed are convinced that investors will be unable to do business in Germany without banking licenses. It remains to be seen whether actual problems will develop in this area. It has, however, been observed that some Anglo-Saxon distressed debt investors are increasingly obtaining stakes in German credit institutions to secure banking licenses for themselves.

In conclusion, it should be said that the results shown provide an interesting inside view of the German distressed debt market from the banks' point of view. It will be exciting to monitor how the German distressed debt market actually develops, and to what extent the banks' assertions are indeed correct.

Part 3: Practical Financial Restructuring Examples – Case Studies

Financial Restructuring
of a Pharmaceutical Company

Karl-J. Kraus, Ralf Moldenhauer

1   The Company

Pharma AG, a stock exchange listed provider of pharmaceutical specialty products, has two business units:

- BU 1: Products for the treatment of diseases (approx. 70% of revenues)

- BU 2: Diagnosis of clinical disease patterns (approx. 30% of revenues)

The company, which has been in business for more than 50 years, manufactures its products in Germany, and distributes them via several domestic and international distribution companies. Sales have increased continuously in recent years.

The root causes of the crisis comprise strategic, structural and operational elements, which are summarized in Fig. 1.

Strategic	• Strategically "all over the place" due to unsuccessful development of new business divisions • Existing pharmaceutical equipment does not allow approval of the products in high price markets • Comprehensive investment program for all business divisions initiated too late • Financing through short-term loans
Structural	• Inadequate management of business divisions and subsidiaries • Acquired companies only partially integrated and minimally controlled • Complex product and client portfolio includes numerous unprofitable small customers as well as items producing minimal sales
Operational	• Over-sized overhead (administration, sales) and consequently excessive structural costs • Excessive fixed capital in inventories and receivables • Inadequate sales performance

Fig. 1: Root causes of the crisis

1.1 Strategic Root Causes of the Crisis

In recent years, the company has been all over the place strategically. To increase its level of diversification, it developed various new activities. To achieve this, the firm made comprehensive investments into the acquisition of companies and in-house developmental activities. These had little effect because the activities were not diligently completed, but were constantly overshadowed by new projects.

At the same time, a strategic disadvantage had an increasingly massive adverse effect on the core business: the production equipment had become obsolete, which made it ever more difficult to market products in high price markets and get them successfully approved. The only way out was to penetrate exotic markets. While the latter are less demanding in terms of product standards, the local pricing levels are also significantly lower. An ambitious investment program was initiated to thoroughly modernize the production facilities. However, the operational cash flow could not cover the investment requirements, thus outside capital was obtained to finance the project (see Fig. 2). This bank liability was however not structured in relation to the long-term investment, but was almost exclusively financed via short-term loan structures.

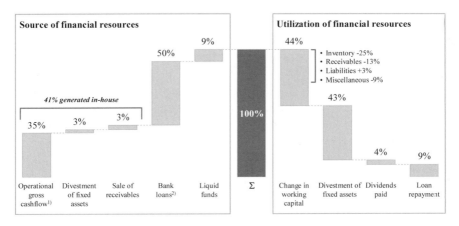

1) Annual profit + non-cash extraordinary expense + depreciation + adjusted pension accruals
2) Incl. leasing

Fig. 2: Four-year capital flow overview

1.2 Structural Root Causes of the Crisis

Given their successful history, the business divisions of the subsidiaries were inadequately controlled. True group controlling simply did not occur, so that the individual companies developed their own style with less than optimal results for the group as a whole. As a consequence, the newly acquired businesses were inadequately integrated with no synergies being created.

1.3 Operational Root Causes of the Crisis

At the operational end, Pharma AG's cost structure was no longer competitive and the allocated working capital had reached a dimension that left no room for an attractive return on capital. At the heart of the problem were two headquarters divisions: administration and sales were over-sized, causing excessive structural costs (about 10% of the total revenues). The business had simultaneously generated a high demand for working capital (inventories and receivables) over the past few years. While an increase in sales was one of the reasons, inadequate receivables management was another. The sales organization was scarcely held accountable for incoming payments. The high inventory levels were the result of decentralized warehousing in Germany (five warehouses); separate warehouses at nine different international distribution companies and inventories designed to cover long periods of time along the entire production chain.

2 The Components of the Restructuring Concept

The structures of pharmaceutical companies are cost-intensive due to comprehensive regulations, as well as essential research and development (R&D) activities. Most of the expenses are fixed costs. Assets usually bind significant investments, and a huge infrastructure must be in place (R&D, clinical research, approvals, quality control, production, sales, logistics, etc.) in order to offer what the market demands.

In addition to standard cost cutting measures, this industry must also take the problem of critical mass into account: the required basic structure can only be operated economically if a critical revenue level is attained. This means that increased sales are a key component in restructuring, and by far the most important earnings lever. The restructuring and strategic reorientation program developed based on these insights can thus be divided into three components (see Fig. 3):

1. Strategic reorientation driving long-term success potential

2. Structural optimization with a medium-term effect

3. Operational efficiency increases that yield short-term success

		Contents	Effect
1	**Strategic re-orientation**	• Forfeit fringe business • Enforce production investment program • Partner search primarily for target market entry • Enforce new product licensing • Focus on attractive segments in BUs	Long-term
2	**Structural optimization**	• Integrate subsidiaries • Centralize logistics	Medium-term
3	**Operational efficiency boost**	• Manage working capital (inventory, receivables) • Reduce costs in Germany (HR, materials, other costs) • Increase profits of foreign companies • Reduce complexity (products/customers) • Increase sales	Short-term

Fig. 3: The components of the restructuring concept

In terms of its strategic reorientation, Pharma AG focused its resources on two business divisions. Non-core activities were sold and the income from these sales was invested in development of the core business.

To improve its market positioning, Pharma AG continued to invest in its new pharmaceutical production, given that only the availability of high-quality products and sales in high price markets would secure Pharma AG's future sustainably. Moreover, thanks to higher returns that translated into significant production cost reductions, these assets had a very positive impact on earnings. To increase the critical mass, cooperation with another pharmaceutical company of about the same size was planned with the objective of facilitating market launches in target markets. Critical mass was further increased through the licensing of new products.

The introduction of centralized logistics yielded significant structural optimization. Operating fewer warehouses translated into a higher level of efficiency, and the introduction of a European logistics system increased the percentage of central warehouse deliveries. Another key restructuring lever was the consequential reduction of complexities via minimum quantity surcharges and minimum quantity requirements, as well as targeted product line adjustments.

The operational efficiency optimization comprised working capital management, general cost cutting, and a sales-up project aiming at stabilizing revenues. A uniform inventory reduction concept (back-up inventory, throughput times, master agreements, etc.) was incorporated into the working capital management. Stringent receivables management measures (persistent collection activities, creditworthiness checks, etc.) were introduced simultaneously. At headquarters, a comprehensive cost-reduction program affecting human resources, material, and other operational costs, was launched. The entire concept was completed by a sales-up project aimed at increased revenues and more stable earnings.

In the very first year of restructuring, reductions of about 10% of total costs had already been initiated and positive effects on profits were reported in the P&L. For the following years, additional measures with an effect of about 5% on revenues had been defined; which were successively introduced. Simultaneously, working capital was reduced by approximately 8% on the balance sheet total in the first year, while the investment program was reduced or delayed for total savings of about 10% without any adverse impact on performance. All of this was achieved in an unexpectedly weak market environment.

3 Financial Restructuring

After the operational and strategic restructuring of the company had been largely finalized, preparations for financial restructuring were undertaken. The practical and temporal logic was based on two factors: on one hand positive development of the business and the successful restructuring phase had provided a solid foundation for refinancing. On the other hand, restructuring financing was set to run out in the medium term. New financing principally hinges on capital providers (equity and outside capital) regaining their trust in the company's competitive and value creation capabilities after a crisis. This prerequisite was being met thanks to earnings improvements and available liquidity, as well as consistent implementation of the defined restructuring measures, although revenues had declined. The bridge financing obtained for corporate restructuring had been limited to a period of two years to keep the sense of urgency at the company high, and to prevent the enterprise from being overloaded with crisis-specific credit terms and conditions. In this context we would like to note that the financing term is frequently the result of a compromise between the various banks involved, given that different institutions assess their loan commitment differently based on the individual amount granted, the respective collateralization, willingness to take risks, and other criteria. To this end, the bridge terms are only rarely entirely based on the entrepreneurial requirements, but are primarily driven by the interests of the financiers.

Like the company, the credit institutions (go-banks) that remained long-term oriented had an interest in closing the refinancing transaction completely and with adequate time reserve prior to expiration of the existing loans, in order to prevent financial emergencies, including termination of individual commitments. The intended refinancing model comprises three key objectives:

- Term-congruent funding

- Ensuring of growth and investment financing

- Coverage of short-term liquidity requirements resulting from the exit of individual banks

The anticipated result was an investment grade (BBB) and dissolution of the existing bank pool (since the outbreak of the crisis, a collateral-trust agreement had been in place between the financing banks and the company). Fig. 4 provides an overview of the objectives of the financing concept.

Action required	Cover financial needs	Improve financial structure	

Contents	Cover liquidity needs to 2006/07
	
	• Strategic reorientation
	  – Complete investment program
	  – Penetrate European market, primarily through development of sales, approvals, etc. (~EUR 20-30 m)
	
	• Repay banks due to expiration of pool contract by end 2004 – exit of selected banks (~ EUR 20 m)
		Eliminate existing imbalance in balance sheet and optimize future financial structure, taking financial needs into account
		
		• Finance long-term binding investments long-term
		
		• Finance remaining financial needs through short-term loans
			Objective
			
			• Attain investment levels
			• Dissolve collateral trust pool

Volume	~ EUR 40-50 m	~ EUR 50 m	

Fig. 4: The objectives of the financing concept

The need for *term-congruent financing* arose from the previous practice of the business to finance a comprehensive investment program (volume more than EUR 100 million over ten years), which had been in place since 1998, entirely through operational cash flow. In recent years, given earnings declines and increased working capital tie-up, operational cash flow had been insufficient to fully fund the investment needs. The resulting liquidity requirements were covered through extensions of short-term credit lines (see Fig. 2). The wide gap between the due dates – terms of one year for assets that would be with a service life of more than ten years – was one of the factors that triggered the crisis.

The enterprise had successfully developed several research projects in one of its subsidiaries (to Phase 1 or 2).[1] In order to accelerate the further development of these projects to market maturity, additional expenses for human resources and studies totaling about EUR 30 million were required over a period of five years. The added value to be gained from these additional investments was three to five

---

[1] The development of pharmaceuticals is divided into various phases (1 through 3 as well as pre-clinical), which describe the extent and contents of required trials and document the respective findings on the efficacy of the active ingredients. The phase can consequently also be utilized to assess the risk profile of the development project.

times that amount. In addition to *securing these development projects financially*, the focus had to be placed on ensuring additional *core business growth* in keeping with the financing of the business-congruent working capital allocation (primarily receivables and inventories), as well as retention of the investment program, due to the fact that entry into new markets hinged on the quality attained by new production facilities.

Based on statements made by some of the banks upon execution of the collateral-trust agreement (CTA) it had to be anticipated that the refinancing concept would only be endorsed by some of the credit institutions involved. The reduction of the credit line inherent in *the exit of individual banks* (exit banks) was not tolerable given the existing liquidity planning, so that adequate liquidity had to be ensured for the remainder of the CTA term. In this context it also had to be taken into account that the remaining credit institutions would probably not accept a simple exit of some of the banks. Consequently, a model that would be persuasive for all stakeholders had to be developed that would provide compelling reasons to support the exit of some and the continued engagement of others.

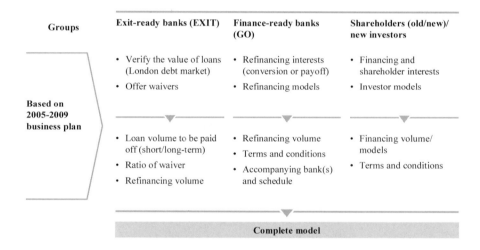

Fig. 5: Overview of methods

3.1 Method and Content

The activities began about six months prior to expiration of existing financial contracts, in order to ensure that ample time for negotiations with existing and new capital providers would be available. Negotiations were based on a comprehensive business plan covering a period of five years that laid out the economic effects of all measures (investment program, development projects, restructuring, etc.), and simultaneously described and explained how the value and development of the company were secured. Based on this long-term business plan (continuation of existing financing and its assumed structure) specific components had to be developed for the individual interest groups (see Fig. 5).

The core elements of this refinancing concept were:

- Conversion of some of the operational material loans into long-term loans, as well as adapting terms in existing leasing contracts to the economic life-cycle of the equipment,

- Solicitation of fresh money through a capital increase,

- Repayment of bank loans with credit institutions ready to exit.

These core elements were based on the following presumptions/overall conditions:

1. The remaining banks will not increase their existing financing volume and will not take over lines from the exiting banks.

2. In the first year, the liquidity influx from the capital increase will be balanced against a significantly lower consumption amount, so that the funds not required during this time period will become available to repay the loans of the exiting banks.

3. Additional liquid funds generation as a result of targeted working capital measures was possible and feasible.

Even as the concept-related work was being performed – such as preparation of a financing concept, formulating the equity story, execution of a company valuation, execution of a rating, etc.; preliminary negotiations took place with all capital provider groups (banks, existing shareholders, and potential shareholders), to arrive at the maximum possible consensus for the financing concept, and to take the interests of all stakeholders into account promptly. Thus it was possible to respond flexibly to the changing requirements of individual capital providers, which in turn were driven by the requirements of others. On the other hand the interests of the company were considered thanks to the generation of an objectives catalog, which summarized the goals that would be achieved through the new financing concept. Thus for example target capital structures were determined in order to maintain an investment grade rating (see Fig. 6).

In addition to coming up with the concept, Roland Berger Strategy Consultants assumed the role of a moderator to facilitate and accelerate the entire process. RBSC's function was not restricted to managing the negotiations; it also required providing pragmatic approaches to solutions enabling a return to negotiations when they sometimes reached an impasse. As the negotiations progressed, this translated into comprehensive concept adaptations – which, as the process continued, sometimes had to be reversed in keeping with an iterative solution process.

All of this had an impact on the business plan, as well as on the earnings and liquidity situation of the stakeholders. Parallel to the bank negotiations, activities aimed at attracting private equity companies, as well as preparation of the data room and all related tasks, were being performed. A limited number of providers of new forms of financing (e.g. mezzanine capital) were simultaneously being solicited.

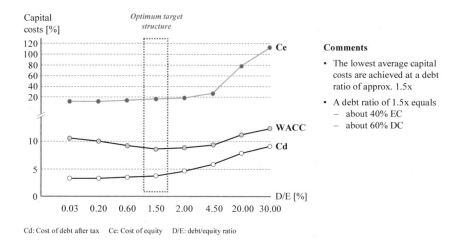

Cd: Cost of debt after tax   Ce: Cost of equity   D/E: debt/equity ratio

Fig. 6: Target capital structure and rating

3.2   Results

As a result of the project, Pharma AG received financing based on its future requirements, but the content of such funding partially deviates from the original concept. However, this is indeed a standard outcome of negotiations between diverging interest groups, and is necessary to conclude an agreement. In particular it was not possible to get a capital increase placement from institutional investors, given that the private equity companies found the respective conditions unattractive. The primary reasons were:

- The company is listed on the stock exchange

- Only a (qualified) minority share can be attained

- The majority of the company is still owned by the founding family

- The enterprise is not large enough (revenues around EUR 300 million)

Almost all of the creditor requirements were being met. Exiting banks waived a significant amount of receivables; the remaining banks converted about 50% of their short-term loans into long-term loans (seven-year terms). The planned capital increase will probably still be attained through placements of shares held by small investors, since the stock price has improved about 550% in approximately 2.5 years. In addition to these measures the anticipated redemption of the existing financing could be deferred to ensure the required liquid funds were available for discharging the obligations to the exiting banks. In this context it is noteworthy that initially about 40% of the banks announced their exit from the engagement for various reasons (e.g. changed orientation of the bank's business, cessation of their corporate banking program, loss of trust, etc.). However in the end only half of this number did indeed exit.

In summary, it is safe to assume that the company, thanks to the new financing concept, does meet the requirements for successful future development. Although the current refinancing solution does not cover a capital increase, the prerequisites for a respective capital market measure have been significantly improved.

3.3   Lessons Learned

In summary, the following success factors have been identified that can be applied to tasks equivalent to those that were required to address the situation at Pharma AG:

- A comprehensive understanding of the overall value chain of the company is the basis for putting together a business plan

- The business plan should be modularly structured to allow transformation of concept modifications into short-term financial effects for all stakeholders

- An understanding of the requirements that every stakeholder places on the concept, to enable presentation of a sustainable concept in the early stages of the project

- Negotiations should be moderated by a consultant who takes on the role of a mediator

- Alternatives should be developed to generate time and content pressure.

Reorganization and Capital Market – Growth Financing Shores Up the Restructuring Process

Sascha Haghani, Maik Piehler

1 Introduction

At the very latest since the 90s, restructuring projects have become important tools for German companies. Especially the construction and retail industries are suffering in an environment dominated by difficult economic conditions. In this kind of scenario it is no longer sufficient to focus restructuring efforts on operational and structural areas. On the contrary, to secure the future development of a business, sustainable strategies must be compiled and the strategic path of progression must be safeguarded financially.

Fendox Group is a building material wholesaler. Since mid-2001, Roland Berger Strategy Consultants has been commissioned to restructure the Fendox Group. This case study describes the comprehensive restructuring concept implemented by Fendox Group. In addition to the traditional restructuring concept (operational, structural. and strategic measures), we will focus particularly on introducing the financial restructuring program.

2 Initial Situation

Fendox Group is a wholesaler in the construction industry and has a market share of 10% in its industry, turning over around EUR 500 million p.a., which makes it the European market leader. In 2000, more than 70% of these revenues were produced in Germany. Fendox Group comprises 20 independent international companies worldwide, two independent German subsidiaries, and the German parent company (hereinafter referred to as Fendox Domestic). Fendox Domestic's competitors are a few large cross-regional wholesalers, and a handful of small regional dealers. A small number of manufacturers dominate the market. Fig. 1 provides an cverview of the relative market shares of manufacturers and wholesalers.

118

Manufacturers

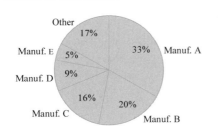

Dealers

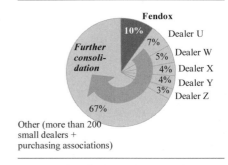

- Small number of established large manufacturers
- The two largest manufacturers of window hardware (A and B) cover half of the market

- Large number of active small dealers and associations
- Fendox is Germany's largest construction hardware dealer and the European market leader; the company is the only dealer with nation-wide coverage in Germany
- Further consolidation is a consequence of a declining market

Fig. 1: Overview of the market shares of manufacturers and wholesalers in Germany, status 2000

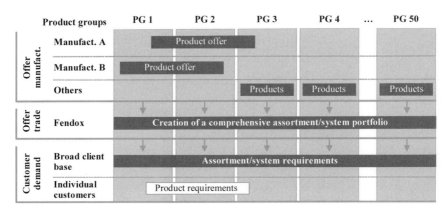

Comments

- Manufacturers each offer many products from individual product groups
- Wholesaler compiles a well-rounded, comprehensive assortment/system portfolio from the products offered (Fendox utilizes 50 product groups)
- Detailed logistics and sales are more effective if performed by wholesalers than by manufacturers thanks to the former's core competencies
- Manufacturers can only compile assortments through the integration of a trading function

Fig. 2: Portfolio creation, distribution and logistics functions of Fendox Domestic

Industrial manufacturers (industrial processors in the construction industry) as well as artisans and small dealers make up the Fendox Domestic customer roster. As a connecting link between manufacturers and customers, Fendox Domestic is primarily taking on a portfolio creating, distribution and logistics function. It is bundling various product offerings from individual suppliers into one product assortment portfolio. In addition, it handles the nation-wide distribution and shipment of merchandise (see Fig. 2).

Fendox Domestic's distribution network had grown historically and was highly decentralized. Nationwide, the company operated 30 distribution sites; all of these sites included a warehouse. These warehouses were considered the company's primary competitive edge in their relations with regional accounts.

Until the mid-90s, the entire Fendox Group saw positive development. Due to large revenue increases in the aftermath of German reunification (for example, thanks to the construction boom in the new Federal States), Fendox Domestic expanded its capacities accordingly. The end of the German construction boom, which came in the late nineties, dampened this positive development.

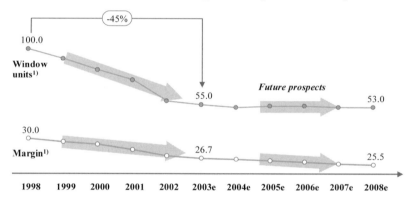

Comments

- Dramatic market decline since 1998 (-45% within five years)
- Prices remain under pressure in a difficult market environment
- Earnings situation very negative
- Very strong cost pressure – rationalization potential virtually exhausted
- Increasing onslaught because of hardware from Eastern Europe and China/Asia
- Market recovery not on the horizon

1) Indicated

Fig. 3: Market situation for windows in Germany

While international operations and the German subsidiaries produced stable and profitable growth, the revenues of Fendox Domestic began to decline in 1998. As evident in Fig. 3, revenues and margins decrease significantly along the entire value chain. Given that the market has lost about 45% in just five years (from 1998 to 2003), this downward spiral will probably continue in the years to come.

Fendox Domestic did not adapt its capacities to the sustained decline of the construction industry and produced its first losses in 2000. Initially a mere earnings crisis, the situation had worsened by mid-2001, and led to an acute liquidity crisis.

3 The Restructuring Process

The existing management recognized the fact that the Fendox Group was in the midst of a crisis by mid-2001. Credit lines (mostly credit lines with seven banks) were increasingly being utilized – Fendox had entered the state of an acute liquidity crisis. Banks initially gave management until fall 2001 to come up with an acceptable restructuring concept. A bank pool was established to provide liquidity until a financing decision was made based on this concept. This prevented individual banks from terminating their respective credit lines – for this reason, relevant decisions had to be made unanimously.

3.1 Identified Root Causes of the Crisis

In the first week of the restructuring project a rough analysis of the internal and external situation of Fendox Domestic was performed. Five primary root causes of the crisis were identified:

1. Thus far, *marketing had been non-differentiated,* due to the fact that the company did not have a product/marketing strategy. Fendox Domestic delivered everything to everybody. A clear focus on profitable product/market segments could not be identified.

2. In recent years a high level of *complexity* had been created in terms of *suppliers* (35% of the suppliers produced 99% of the revenues)**,** *products* (13% of the products generated 90% of the revenues), and *customers* (30% of the clients brought in 94% of gross profit).

3. As a result of the integration of smaller companies, which had occurred in previous years, *the organization was also highly complex*. The *structure* was dominated by 30 distribution and warehousing sites all over Germany, comprehensive administrative divisions, and a large board. This decentralized organization also resulted in very different *processes* at the numerous sites. The ability to control the company was therefore very restricted.

4. The complexity the company had created in terms of its own organization, as well as the business model translated into a *high level of capital tie-up.* The 30 warehouses carried a high percentage of redundant *inventories* – also due

to the minimum quantities required. A lack of inventory management and decentralized planning created high inventories of non-moving and slow-moving products (with in-stock quantities to last more than 18 months). About a third of the entire inventory consisted of non-moving and slow-moving products.

A similar picture emerged in the analysis of *receivables.* Almost 30% of receivables had been overdue for more than 150 days. Moreover, due to the difficult market situation and the lack of collections monitoring, many receivables defaulted due to corporate insolvencies.

5.   The *corporate culture* was dominated by bureaucratic structures. Employees developed very few ideas autonomously and rarely raised critical questions. Innovation was not being promoted; an entrepreneurial spirit simply did not exist. Staff initiative was not rewarded. Sales staff, for example, received a high fixed salary and virtually no performance-based compensation.

3.2   The Classical Restructuring Concept

Based on detailed analyses of the internal and external business scenario and an assessment of the future development of the market, a restructuring concept was drafted. The concept primarily comprised strategic reorientation, structural and operational measures, as well as supporting activities. The required medium-term financial restructuring was initiated through a search for investors. However, the initial focus was on strategic, structural, and operational issues.

3.2.1   Strategic Reorientation

A principal decision on the future strategic orientation and development of the entire Fendox Group had to be made. Concentration on profitable and future-oriented customer and product segments was at the heart of the concept. Given that in contrast to the domestic market, the international market is expected to continue to grow strongly in years to come (see Fig. 4), these activities were to be boosted.

A more specific analysis of the different markets revealed that the international market could be developed much more profitably than the domestic market. One of the main reasons was the fact that the foreign markets as such were less complex in terms of manufacturers and wholesalers, as well as in terms of the diversification of systems offered.

Given that the majority of all relevant manufacturers are domiciled in Germany, all service the German market, but only a few are actually active internationally. Local manufacturers play only a minor role. A similar picture emerged in an evaluation of the wholesalers. Internationally, there are only a selected few servicing the market, while Germany is penetrated by innumerable, i.e. smaller, dealers (see Fig. 5).

122

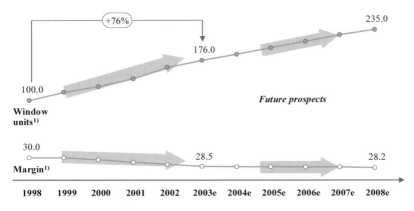

Comments

- Stable growth in recent years – continued solid growth anticipated
- Growth must be secured through financing and development of new markets
- Increasingly higher risks in terms of international growth due to new cultures, values, distances
- Margin eroding in Eastern and Western Europe due to cannibalization tendencies (e.g. Poland)

1) Indicated

Fig. 4: Market development for windows (international)

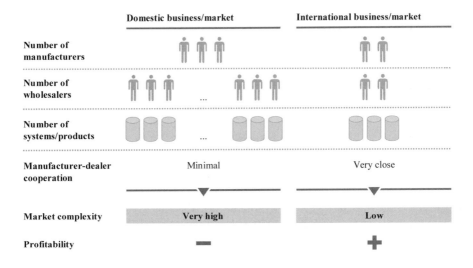

Fig. 5: Characteristics and profitability of the domestic and international markets

Given the much smaller number of active parties, cooperation with the individual value levels was far less complex in the international markets than it was in Germany. Closer cooperation and coordination with manufacturers became an integral part of Fendox' domestic strategy. Other elements of the domestic strategy were consolidation of Fendox Domestic, as well as stronger positioning of the domestic subsidiaries that had already been successful in profitable niche markets.

3.2.2   Structural Measures

One of the critical components addressed by the structural measures was the *reduction of distribution sites* from 30 (including administration) to 12 locations (without administrative functions) plus corporate headquarters. All administrative functions (purchasing, accounting/controlling, receivables and inventory management) were to be consolidated at corporate headquarters. The objective was homogenization of processes, elimination of unused capacities, as well as cost reductions and reduced capital tie-up through intensified centralization.

For the purpose of structural streamlining, a significant *reduction of the logistics sites* was targeted. This move, which would reduce the 30 active warehousing locations to 6, hinged on introducing a new logistics concept. Utilizing a hub-and-spokes system, nation-wide distribution was to be realized via 14 transfer points (see Fig. 7). The transfer points would be supplied by six active warehousing locations on a daily basis and handle final distribution. They would not carry any inventory of their own. In addition to cost reductions, this system was to reduce the minimum inventories while also ensuring 100% availability through facilitated inventory management.

These nation-wide structural measures were further enhanced by introducing a *category management organization*. Use of targeted portfolio management tools, promotes distribution of products that drive up margins and revenues. Complete portfolio management is one of the main pillars of the business model and was to be concentrated in a single unit. This unit was also entrusted with the responsibility for purchase terms and payment term negotiations with suppliers.

Via centralization, central *receivables and inventory management functions* were created as well. In addition to ongoing implementation and monitoring of credit limits, as well as inventory planning, targeted measures aimed at reducing overdue receivables and sale of non-moving and slow-moving products are to be realized as well.

3.2.3   Operational Measures

The operational measures that were installed in concert with the structural measures primarily involved human resources, other operational expenses, inventory, and receivables. These measures were closely linked with the structural modifications. A large percentage of the reductions in *human resources* were achieved by closing facilities, for example. The elimination of *inventory and receivables* is to be driven by adapted processes and centralizing the respective control function. Moreover, any purchases that were not absolutely necessary were avoided and the general comfort level was lowered. The full-color employee newsletter, for example, was abolished. Instead, employees now receive regular e-mail updates that are also more current. This tool could simultaneously be used as a faster and more direct information and control medium in the restructuring process.

3.3   Implementation of the Restructuring Concept

The Fendox Group restructuring concept, which was developed by mixed teams, was presented to the financing banks in the fall of 2001. As a result, the banking pool committed to continue financing for a period of just under a year. This commitment was made subject to fast implementation of the concept presented. Medium-term financial restructuring was continually monitored through an investors' process, which initially focused on obtaining proof of Fendox Groups capability to deliver in terms of economic performance. By late 2002, the company was able to document definitive successes in the individual restructuring modules.

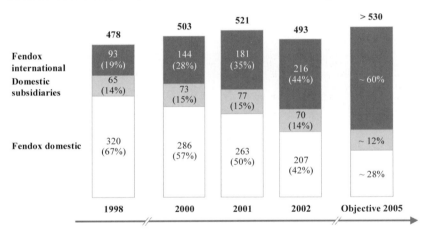

Fig. 6: Revenue distribution Fendox Group 1998-2005e

3.3.1   Strategic Approach

Fendox Group successfully launched its strategic reorientation on the Group level. The revenue shares of the profitable international business could be significantly increased from 28% in 2000 to 44% in 2002 (see Fig. 6). The next objective was to catapult the international share to approximately 60% by 2005. The business of

Fendox Domestic was consolidated as unprofitable customers and products were left behind. Perpetuated by the continued decline of the domestic market, Fendox Domestic's share of revenues fell from 57% in 2000 to only 42% by fiscal year 2002. In the years to come, the domestic market is expected to further decrease in terms of significance for the Group. The domestic subsidiaries were able to keep their share in the Group's revenues fairly stable. Better positioning in more profitable niche markets and initiation of earnings improvement programs allowed the subsidiaries to actually improve their earnings despite declining sales.

Streamlining of the logistics structure   **Introduction hub-and-spokes system**

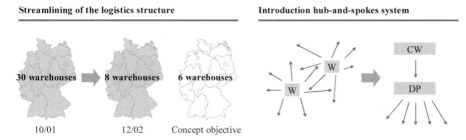

| 30 warehouses | 8 warehouses | 6 warehouses |
| 10/01 | 12/02 | Concept objective |

Comments

- 30 warehouses were cut down to 8 active warehouses through the creation of six central warehouses, a special warehouse and an export warehouse
- Key accounts were linked to electronic material management interfaces
- Significant supply problems overcome by mid-year thanks to closer relationships with suppliers and better alignment
- Introduction of a hub-and-spokes system
    - Former logistics structure was based on 30 regional warehouse sites
    - New logistics structure features six central warehouses (CW) and regional distribution points (DP) for detailed distribution
    - Significant reduction of required minimum inventory quantities thanks to fewer warehouse sites
    - Delivery times can still be warranted

Fig. 7: Structural changes in logistics

3.3.2   Operational and Organizational Measures

Warehouse operations were reduced from 30 to 8 sites. A hub-and-spoke system was also introduced – ordered merchandise is now distributed to transfer points overnight and delivered to the respective customers from these locations (see Fig. 7). This change yielded significant inventory and cost reductions while maintaining a high level of availability for optimum customer service.

The number of *distribution sites* could be reduced from 30 to 17. A further consolidation into 13 locations had been planned (see Fig. 8). To increase the profitability of small German customers, they were assigned to telephone sales to be handled by sales admin personnel. A selective price increase for C and D customers, with average 10-20%, was also implemented. Consequently the previously

126

unprofitable C and D customers are now producing positive margins. Moreover, a special task force that prospects for new accounts has been established to gain market share.

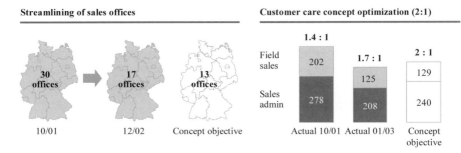

Streamlining of sales offices

10/01 → 12/02 → Concept objective

Customer care concept optimization (2:1)

Field sales / Sales admin

Actual 10/01 — Actual 01/03 — Concept objective

Comments

- Elimination of 13 sales offices (reduced from 30 to 17), consolidation of the sales groups in the remaining offices
- Efficiency increased thanks to active inside sales consulting for German customers (telephone sales/call center)
- Sales controlling for revenue management established
- Measures to reactivate lost revenues defined
- Task force for new client prospecting appointed
- Ratio of sales admin and field staff optimized

Fig. 8: Structural changes in sales

Category management was launched successfully. Product diversity was cut by about 15%; the number of suppliers was cut by about 50% (see Fig. 9). The core business could be focused on 40% fewer items. A significant reduction in complexity was achieved.

The structural changes and the centralization of planning allowed Fendox Domestic to cut inventories from EUR 70 million to EUR 45 million. After a brief setback in mid-2002, product availability could once again be increased in 2003 (see Fig. 10). This was achieved primarily through closer coordination with suppliers and the introduction of a new, active inventory management system.

Thanks to the restructuring measures, the company was in a position to stabilize its liquidity situation, which had been a looming threat, by mid-2001 and was able to improve it by the end of fiscal year 2002. The regained confidence of the banks ensured the continued availability of credit lines at the previous level. Despite declining market development in 2002 and 2003, slight market share gains could ultimately be realized. In the perception of customers and suppliers, Fendox Domestic has also regained stability and is considered to be an established reliable partner. The stronger growth in profitable international markets contributed to this outcome. After wiping the slate clean of old liabilities (e.g. inventory and receivables write-downs, amortizations of stakes in companies) in 2001 and 2002, the consolidated results of the entire Fendox Group had been considerably improved.

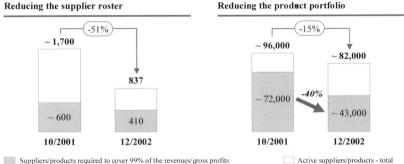

Comments

- Revenue concentration on 43,000 core products (main business can now be covered with 40% fewer products)
- Category management organization and product manager introduced
- Category management is profit-oriented
- Core suppliers per product group have been defined
- Core assortments have been defined and are now being focused on
- Suppliers with low volume blocked and number of items reduced by 14,000
- Gross profits improved thanks to supplier negotiations and purchasing coordination
- Inventories reduced by EUR 29 m (-37%) thanks to active inventory management

Fig. 9: Structural changes thanks to the introduction of category management

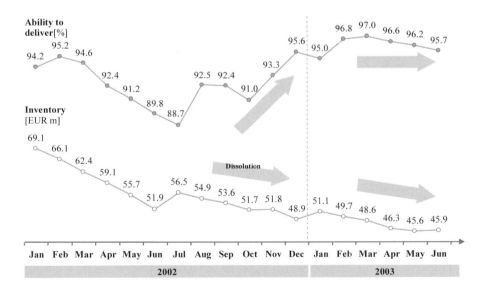

Fig. 10: Development of product availability and inventory

3.4 Financial Restructuring

In 2003, the Fendox Group had made significant progress in the traditional areas of restructuring, and a turnaround was imminent. However, in particular the strategic goals could not be fully pursued. The reason was the limited balance sheet and financial flexibility of the Fendox Group as a result of the years of crisis it had just been through.

3.4.1 Challenges After Classic Restructuring

After completing the main phase of traditional restructuring, the Fendox Group was confronted with five major financial challenges:

1. The annual *interest burden* of about 3% is very high for a trading company. In addition to international subsidiary growth financing, one of the primary causes was the historical loss funding of the crisis years, in particular for the domestic business. Outside debts in 2003 totaled about 35% of sales volume.

2. The accrued losses from the domestic business have consumed the *equity capital of the major domestic subsidiary*. After ranking rescissions of Fendox-Holding had already economically "healed" the negative balance sheet equity capital, no further ranking rescissions were possible. This meant that the company was caught in a legally difficult equity capital scenario.

3. Given that the profit outlook for the major domestic subsidiary was extremely limited due to the enormous interest burden (it was responsible for more than half of the total outside debts of the Fendox Group), in a persistently difficult domestic market, it was expected that provisions *for depreciation* would have to be made in 2003 in the Fendox-Holding balance sheet for this company. This means that there was an associated approximate 12% burden on the holding's equity capital ratio (the equity capital ratio of Fendox-Holding had dropped to a mere 25% by 2002). A further reduction was simply not acceptable.

4. Growth of the more profitable international companies had to continue at a subdued rate. The majority of foreign earnings were utilized for continuing liquidity transfers to Germany in order to satisfy the high interest burden. *Growth funding in the foreign markets* was consequently greatly limited and strategic development of the entire Fendox Group was hampered.

5. Given the above four factors, the existing financing circle *could not expect* repayment on the loans that had been granted. The willingness to further accompany the Fendox Group differed significantly between the various financial institutions. This led to tension within the banking pool, and had an adverse impact on its relationship with the Fendox Group; in some cases this hampered the operational business.

In mid-2003 these five issues prompted reinforcement of the investor search process, which had already been initiated in 2002, and development of a concept for financial restructuring of the Fendox Group.

3.4.2 Approaches for Financial Restructuring

Over a period of twelve months, a large number of potentially interested parties in Germany and abroad were contacted by a commissioned investment bank as part of the investor process. However, less than five financial investors expressed an interest in an engagement, while the strategic investors who had been solicited were not interested at all. By fall 2003 a final offer had been received from a financial investor, which was however rejected due to the inability of the banking pool to arrive at a unanimous vote. The key element of the investor's proposal was a cash settlement with the entire banking pool at a relatively low quota.

While investor negotiations continued, several additional negotiations with potentially interested parties were being pursued in the company's environment. The objective of these negotiations was to solicit capital shareholder arrangements or cooperative scenarios, for example.

Since neither the investor process nor any of the parallel negotiations yielded any satisfactory solutions for the challenges that had been identified, an integrated recapitalization concept was pursued.

3.4.3 Development and Implementation of the Recapitalization Concept

Immediately after the banking pool had turned down the investor's offers in the fall of 2003, a rough recapitalization concept was introduced. The principles for recapitalization agreed on were the following:

- *Sustainable contribution of all stakeholders to the restructuring process*: after contributions from employees, suppliers, customers, and shareholders had taken effect in the previous restructuring processes, financial institutions and shareholders (once again) were now expected to make more contributions.

- *Abolishment of the banking pool idea*: given the tensions within the banking pool and the diverging attitudes of the individual institutions, they were to decide at their own discretion whether they would continue to accompany the Fendox Group.

- *(Partial) foregoing of income by the exiting banks:* institutions who were no longer willing to accompany the Fendox group were to forego (part of) their loan volume for the benefit of the Fendox Group.

- *Parity contributions by the remaining banks and shareholders/investors:* given that new equity capital (fresh money) also improves the position of those institutions continuing to provide financing, they were to convert an amount equivalent to their loans into equity capital (debt equity swap).

- *Partially success-based compensation of the remaining institutions:* the banks continuing to provide financing were to participate in positive development of the business (in addition to their shares from the debt equity swap).

- *Improved equity options for remaining institutions:* given that even in the past individual institutions had pursued the tradability of their loans, an opportunity would now be created to sell parts of the loan portfolio to reduce the risk position.

The development and negotiation of a recapitalization concept was resolved on the basis of these principles. A period of about three months was allotted for negotiations, during which two core bank meetings (with three selected banks) took place. In the course of this period, numerous investor negotiations were completed and more than 40 versions of a basic model that had been pre-negotiated with the investors and core banks were presented to the banking pool in early 2004. The basic elements comprised:

- A capital reduction/cut to adapt Fendox-Holding capital stock to the economic equity capital situation after the required write-downs had been applied.

- Confirmed influx of more than EUR 15 million in equity capital (fresh money) from investors.

- Pay-off of individual bank liabilities with a nominal value of more than EUR 50 million with a significant rebate in favor of the Fendox Group (the pay-off was counter-financed by fresh money).

- Conversion of outside capital liabilities of the banks continuing to provide financing into equity capital (volume equivalent to the influx of fresh money).

- Conversion of another EUR 50 million in outside capital debt into stock exchange suitable, modifiable participation capital with variable interest depending on the Fendox Group's business development.

Once the banking pool's approval of this recapitalization concept had been obtained, the legal (stock company law) and technical implementation could be initiated. It took about ten months, including a shareholder meeting and execution of the capital measures, as well as the application for the stock exchange listing, to develop and implement the recapitalization of the Fendox Group.

The financial challenges were successfully handled. Moreover, the communication of the recapitalization concept sent a clear signal to the procurement and sales markets of the Fendox Group, which also improved its strategic positioning. The stock price has developed very positively since then as well, and the market capitalization quintupled within a year (includes the implemented capital measures).

4 Conclusions and Outlook

Fendox Domestic gained a lot of ground in just a year and a half of traditional restructuring, and changed considerably. The increasingly competitive environment in a shrinking market made this restructuring process very tough in some areas. Mistakes made in the past could not be completely corrected within this period. Experience has shown that the time required to correct errors frequently is just as long as the time these errors were allowed to wreak havoc.

Most companies who are in these kinds of situations find it difficult to maintain or even expand the required financial flexibility for their continued development. After the successful traditional restructuring, the Fendox Group was in a position to substantially reduce financial burdens from the past and strengthen its financial circle. The respective leeway for continued growth in the profitable international markets could therefore be ensured and the planned domestic market consolidation could be initiated.

Some of the problems that have developed in crisis companies over a long period of time can be corrected only by implementing comprehensive and consistent restructuring processes that prepare the affected company for its return to a successful development. The Fendox Group achieved this thanks to an integral restructuring concept comprising its strategic reorientation, structural and operational measures, as well as an integrated recapitalization concept.

Restructuring and Recapitalization of the HD Co. Group

Michael Blatz, Christian Paul, Julian zu Putlitz

1 Introduction

Just few years ago the tools and the circle of institutions available for financing and recapitalization to companies in reorganization scenarios in Germany were relatively underdeveloped. Financing for restructuring from loan providers was usually granted through the establishment of a banking pool and against the provision of comprehensive collateral in favor of the banking pool. Consequently, existing creditors were generally also the ones granting additional loans. However, in some cases, the provision of fresh money to the company by creditors repeatedly resulted in conflicts of interest within the pool banks – especially if the financial resources were to be utilized for growth purposes; thus further increasing the risk exposure of the financing banks. As a result, the only option open to companies to obtain equity capital, or resources comparable to equity capital, for funding of planned growth was to solicit the, until then not very liquid, and nontransparent, distressed capital market. If they did not pursue that route, growth opportunities could not be taken advantage of.

Since 2002 the distressed capital market has made noticeable progress. The volume of such special financing transactions, as well as the amounts paid out for financing have both increased significantly. The following example shows how innovative financial tools used as alternatives to traditional banking pool financing expand the action radius of companies and financiers, and how structuring appropriate for the situation, and pricing adequate for the risk involved, can make the funding of growth successful in the turnaround process.

2 Initial Situation at the Beginning of the Restructuring Process

HD Co. AG[1] looks back on a long corporate history that saw many changes. Established at the end of the 19th century, the company changed its industry focus and ownership several times in the almost 100 years that followed. In the mid-90s of the 20th century, the enterprise invested immense sums in the expansion of new business segments. To this end, it followed a vision of diversification and focused on industries dominated by medium-sized companies. The objective of this strategic approach was to act as a consolidator in fragmented industries and to establish itself as a market leader within a short period of time. In the course of this development, through acquisitions and organic growth, the group also moved into office solutions, a new business segment focusing on the sale and the provision of technical services for office hardware. In 2000 the HD Co. AG board reevaluated its corporate strategy and decided to withdraw from all other business segments and to concentrate the business focus of the group entirely on the office solutions market.

2.1 Corporate Development of HD Co. Hampered by Group Transformation

The transformation of the HD Co. Group into an office solutions business took almost three years. Those business activities that would cease to be a part of the company were successively sold or liquidated. This massive restructuring is evident in the company's revenue figures during this period: while sales totaled more than EUR 800 million in 2001, they had declined to just above EUR 550 million by 2003, equaling a drop in revenues of more than 30% in just two years. It goes without saying that this thorough reshifting required an immense amount of management capacity, which quite obviously made it almost necessary to neglect operational management of the core business, office solutions. Moreover, the restructuring process left its mark on the enterprise's figures. The post-new-economy era of 2000 to 2003 was a time of few acquisition activities and the prices that could be achieved through M&A transactions frequently fell below the book values of the shares of businesses for sale. Thus HD Co. Group also had to give up stakes at prices below their nominal value, and absorb losses resulting from these sales. Ultimately, the extreme reduction of the group's business volume also resulted in over-dimensional overheads and management structures within the concern that were also too complex for the new organization. Moreover, old balance sheet liabilities, in particular the pension entitlements of former employees, had to be supported by a much smaller operational business foundation.

---

[1] Company name and details changed for reasons of confidentiality.

The consequences of this deep restructuring process were evident in the profit and loss statement (see Fig. 1), as well as in the consolidated balance sheet: the operational EBIT (before pension costs and extraordinary expenses) was close to zero, the cumulative result from ordinary business activities (before extraordinary expenses) of these three years totaled minus EUR 80 million. The annual deficit came in at around EUR 57 million. The concern's equity capital also fell to a minimal 12% of the balance sheet total, and the credit lines available to the company were utilized almost fully on a permanent basis. This caused several of the leading banks providing financing to the group to monitor the company's development continually and diligently.

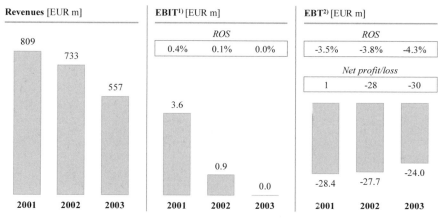

1) Prior to pension expenditures, after company value depreciation
2) After pension expenditures and interest results, not including exceptional items

Fig. 1: The consequences of restructuring as evident in the indices: HD Co. Group, 2001-2003 [EUR million]

However, the HD Co. Group also had good news in store for investors. The newly defined core business delivered constant growth rates in terms of revenues and key performance indicators. The group covered Germany nation-wide, carried strong brands that enjoyed a high level of recognition, and had just recently entered into a strategic partnership with a leading international OEM. In conjunction with this partnership, the OEM had also acquired a substantial portion of the HD Co. AG equity capital and had thus made a clear statement in relation to its interest in the sustained continuation of the cooperation with HD Co. AG. Moreover, HD Co. quickly emerged as one of the most important distributors of this strategic partner in Europe, and produced solid results in office solutions, although operational results were not yet satisfactory for the group as a whole in consideration of its future structure (see Fig. 2).

136

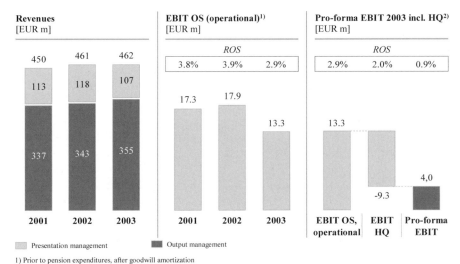

Revenues
[EUR m]

EBIT OS (operational)[1)]
[EUR m]

Pro-forma EBIT 2003 incl. HQ[2)]
[EUR m]

1) Prior to pension expenditures, after goodwill amortization
2) Pro-forma EBIT office solutions incl. company headquarters (HQ)

Fig. 2: The development of the office solutions (OS) business segment, 2001-2003 [EUR million]

2.2 Attractive Market for Output Management, Difficult Market Development for Presentation Management

The office solutions market can roughly be divided in two segments – output management and presentation management. Driven by the emergence of digital technology and functional integration, the market segment has seen a relatively constant development in recent years despite falling prices for hardware, a steady increase in device power, and an increasing commoditization of the equipment. The increasing integration of devices into networks and complete output solutions for individual companies or industries have also caused the office solutions service portion and financing through leasing to grow. In the hardware segment a manageable number of global competitors dominate the market. They supply a large number of independent dealers either directly or through OEM partners. Consolidation has been a key characteristic of the industry for years on both the provider and on the fragmented dealer level.

The presentation management segment has seen lightning-fast developments in both hardware (increase in device sales in the respective market about 20% p.a.) and related services. This development does however go hand in hand with a rapid decline in end user pricing. Based on a market survey performed by a leading international market research firm, the price index in this segment has dropped from its 100% base in 2001 to 46% in 2004, which evidences that the overall market is declining. Moreover, the commoditization of products in the mass market has continued more rapidly than it did in the output management business, so that only a small market segment with regressive tendencies existed for the professional office segment.

In the output management market segment, HD Co. Group was able to point to attractive competitive positioning. Its market share in the key device categories totaled more than 10%. The OEM's product program encompassed primarily devices equipped with digital technology and was therefore at the forefront of technical evolution. In comparison to competitors, the low wear and tear rates of key device components and efficient utilization of consumables gave the devices a measurable cost advantage beyond their typical service life. Service and maintenance agreements with multi-year terms ensured long-term customer relations. The nation-wide presence of service staff allowed the company to offer its customers high service levels.

In the presentation management market segment, HD Co. enjoyed a principally solid competitive position. In addition to well-established brand names, the drive to build a consulting and service-intensive solution business under the company's own brand name would have favored such an assessment. However, at the very onset of the restructuring process, this business segment had to be rated as at risk and contingency plans for possible emergencies were required.

3 An Overview of the Restructuring Concept

In early 2004, the development of the restructuring concept, which created the foundation and prerequisites for implementation of the company's financial restructuring, began. The time proved to be right: the separation from the remaining business activities had been finalized and the group's board was in a position to focus completely on the impending strategic and operational reorientation of the group. Moreover, the strategic partnership with the leading international OEM meant that an important step had been taken on the way to more robust output management activities, both on the product and capital side. Finally, this step also had to be taken given that the first banks were already pressing the company for reductions or even medium-term cessations of their engagements.

The determination of the quantitative and qualitative restructuring objectives at the HD Co. Group began with the minimum requirements in relation to the generation of the capital costs by the group based on a return on capital employed (ROCE) approach. With most of the capital being fixed, an equity capital percentage of 20 in the target structure of the balance sheet, and a capital cost based on the weighted average cost of capital (WACC) of almost 8%, an operational results improvement of about EUR 29 million had to be achieved. Comparing the outcome to international competitor benchmarks, the required operational results improvement had to come in at about EUR 37 million based on an ROCE target of 10% (see Fig. 3). This bandwidth of operational results improvements had to be backed up with structural and operational measures in the restructuring concept, and had to be subsequently implemented.

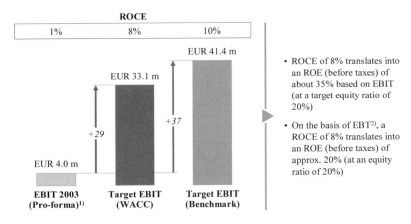

1) Incl. Headquarters, without pension expenditures and extraordinary expense/income
2) Not including exceptional items

Fig. 3: Results improvement needs by success year 2006 [EUR million]

3.1 Structural Reorientation: Letting Go of Non-core Activities and Optimizing the Group Structure

Four starting points were identified in conjunction with the structural reorientation of the HD Co. Group:

1. Streamlining the corporate structure in the output management segment through a company portfolio adjustment

2. Optimization of the site portfolio through closure and mergers of about a third of all company facilities in the output management segment and reduction of related structural costs, as well as consolidation of central functions in the group and retransfer of functions to corporate headquarters

3. Simplification of the company structure in the presentation management segment through merger of companies and elimination of redundant functions, as well as

4. Closure or sale of unprofitable international activities in the presentation management segment in Italy and Egypt

Although the structural reorientation measures called for some deep cuts, most of them could be implemented within 18 months thanks to adequate preparation. The implementation of these measures yielded operational results improvement of about EUR 9.6 million (see Fig. 4).

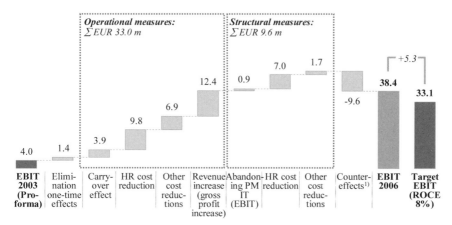

1) Primarily higher HR/miscellaneous costs (EUR 7 m)

Fig. 4: Results improvement through operational and structural measures: results transfer actual 2003 vs. target 2006, HD Co. Group [EUR million]

3.2 Operational Restructuring: Focus on Revenue Increase and Operational Cost Cuts

The operational restructuring began with massive reduction of human resource and material costs that went hand in hand with an increase in revenues and related gross profit. To be able to walk the economic tight rope between deep cost cuts and growth through revenue increases, the planned reduction of staff was performed in several phases. To implement the operational measures, the restructuring concept called for a total of 18 months. The total volume of planned results improvements was approx. EUR 33 million (see Fig. 4).

Thanks to the introduction of effective capacity utilization management, centralized scheduling and optimized territory allocations, the number of potentially redundant field staff and in-house service staff totaled about 15%. In central and decentralized administrative areas, staff reduction potential yielded by streamlining the organization, optimizing process, and the elimination of tasks also totaled 15% of the total administrative capacity. With the assistance of performance benchmarks sales staff reductions of about 8% were identified despite planned increases in the sales output. Overall, across the entire HD Co. Group, staff reductions of more than 10% of the employee capacity and a reduction of personnel expenditures of almost EUR 10 million could be realized. Personnel reduction measures that had already been implemented in the previous year translated into effective savings of about EUR 4 million (so-called carry-over effect).

Other expenditures were reduced by a further approx. EUR 7 million, thanks to three primary effects: first, staff-related material costs could be reduced because of the staff reductions, moreover, effective management and comfort level reductions combined with waived benefits cut additional material costs in central performance areas, and finally, additional cost savings potentials were achieved through group-wide centralization of purchasing for the presentation management segment.

The HD Co. gross profit increase and revenue gains stipulated in the business plan were based primarily on the successive expansion of the installed device basis and related service business in the output management segment. The first key to attain the revenue targets was to safeguard the business with existing customers. Thanks to multi-year leasing and service contract terms, the majority of the turnover to be produced through the management of existing customers in the years to come could be predicted with relative certainty. Based on this concept, several programs were developed and initiated for short-term activation of sales aimed at substantial development of new customer groups, primarily in the industries dominated by medium-sized companies, and at increasing device sales through cross-selling and up-selling. These measures made it possible to adequately support the planned revenue increase of about EUR 32 million, as well as the related increase in gross profit by about EUR 12.4 million.

3.3   The Three Elements of Recapitalization: Capital Increase, Mezzanine Financing, and Structured Financing

The restructuring concept, which was based on operational and structural measures, and the integrated business plan were compiled within six weeks, and subsequently presented to the two banks with the largest loan commitment, the so-called core banks. The objective of this presentation was first to communicate the sustainability of the restructuring concept to the core banks, in order to then determine the next steps in the recapitalization process of the HD Co. Group.

The results of the restructuring concept can be summarized as follows: at the market and product end of the output management segment, the HD Co. Group had secured a stable and safe competitive position and could realize a number of growth opportunities through the ongoing development of existing customers and the development of new client groups.[2] The output management added-value con-

---

[2]   The acquisition of smaller companies in a consolidating market resulted in further growth potential, which was not initially taken into account in the restructuring con-

cept with its established sales channels through direct distribution and retailers, as well as the strategic partnership with the leading international OEM could be assessed as sustainably enforceable. Moreover, detailed, implementation-ready measure plans, or measures that were already underway, aimed at significant cost reductions and a clear improvement of operational performance.

In the much smaller presentation management business segment, this positive future prognosis was fraught with much greater uncertainties. Despite a detailed action program aimed at reduction of operational costs, the business plan contained a number of imponderabilities. Misgivings surfaced, especially in relation to development of sales channels, the prices and margins obtainable in the market, as well as to the related feasibility of realizing sales and gross profit forecasts. Even in the output management segment precautions had to be taken just in case the ambitious revenue increase goals could not be realized.

The restructuring concept therefore did not only encompass a scenario plan that recreated the so-called worst case in the event that business development should fall far short of expectations in the basic forecast, given the premises considered therein. However, even this worst case scenario led to significant improvements of operational results totaling around EUR 17 million p.a., positive earnings before tax of close to EUR 6 million after two years, and a positive, cumulative free cash flow of EUR 3 million. The comprehensive cost-reduction measures also yielded an improvement of the overall HD Co. Group risk profile. After reviewing the restructuring concept at length, the core banks decided to support the reorganization course chosen by the HD Co. board.

More in-depth analyses of the balance sheet and financial structures did however reveal the need for additional action. At the end of 2003, the group's equity capital ratio of 12% was clearly far below the target value of 20%. The group's liquidity forecast also indicated that the liquidity flexibility of the company would be rather limited in the next twelve months, even if the existing credit lines were to remain intact. Therefore no large payments on loans and lines could be made. The group's financing also comprised differing credit facilities of mostly short-term loans with more than 40 different banks, which were also scattered over the entire group. This financial structure made effective cash management in the group more difficult and exposed the overall financing of the corporation to vulnerabilities in the event that individual banks decided to withdraw from the circle of financing banks.

Notwithstanding this problematic creditor constellation, the need to restructure group financing was also evident based on the analyses of typical financial structure indices (see Fig. 5):

---

cept. This additional growth generating option was considered later in the course of the mezzanine capital negotiations.

- The ratio of net bank liabilities to equity capital, the so-called gearing factor, for which a value of 100% is typical in comparable scenarios, was about twice that based on the 2003 consolidated annual report.

- The leverage, defined as the ratio between net bank liabilities and EBITDA, clearly deviated from the target value of between 2 and 3, and came in at a factor of 3.7.

- The interest cover, which describes the ratio between EBITDA and group interest expenditures, was significantly below the target value. The factor in this case was 2.1 vs. a target value between 4 and 5.

- Finally, the group's bank liabilities were almost double that of the indicative target debt level determined by the core banks based on free cash flow.

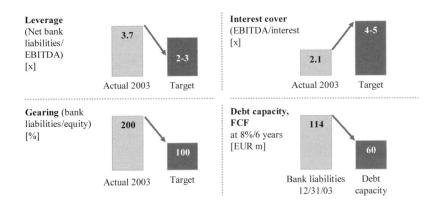

Fig. 5: Divergence of the financial indices from standard market values

These aspects reflected the group financing restructuring requirements of the funding banks, and also emphasized the critical need for an influx of external funding in the amount of at least EUR 23 million in the form of equity capital or equivalent funding. At the same time, the shareholders had imposed restrictions that had to be considered in the overall HD Co. recapitalization concept. This meant, for example, that the leading international OEM could only acquire a limited number of additional HD Co. AG shares within the scope of a capital increase without entering into an acquisition commitment pursuant to §35 Article 2 Sentence 1 WpÜG, and having to file an application for a waiver of a mandatory offer pursuant to § 37 WpÜG with the Bundesanstalt für Finanzdienstleistungsaufsicht (BaFin, Federal Banking Supervising Agency). Taking into account the additional restrictions that had been imposed at the equity capital providers' end, it was evident that the maximum capital increase that could properly be achieved was EUR 17 million. As a result, the company still lacked at least EUR 6 million in equity capital-like funding to inject the required fresh money total of EUR 23 million into HD Co.

To solicit the relatively small remainder and to procure additional financial resources for financing of acquisitions, the board, with the assistance of various specialized financial consultants, initiated a process to enter into negotiations with suitable mezzanine financiers. Notwithstanding the fact that the utilization of these types of financial tools is still somewhat of a rarity in Germany in comparison to the American market, an adequate number of renowned internationally operating mezzanine financiers could be found in a short period of time that showed interest in the transaction. This allowed the board of the HD Co. Group to accelerate the provider selection process and to subsequently focus on the design and alignment of the secondary mezzanine facility with the remaining financing components.

The complexity of this task was considerably influenced by the fact that all of the financing elements hinged on the conditions of the other financing instruments. This made a permanent alignment of the work status with all parties involved in the overall process an absolute necessity and resulted in a lot of time being spent on coordination. Nevertheless, a little more than eight months after the work on the HD Co. Group restructuring concept had begun, a three-element recapitalization that was perfectly synchronized in terms of time and content could be successfully implemented.

The group received an influx of about EUR 17 million through a standard capital increase. This money was used primarily to strengthen the equity capital base of the group, and was primarily utilized to pay off smaller loans with short terms. A substantial portion of the capital increase was provided by the leading international OEM that increased its stake in the HD Co. AG to a figure just below the threshold value of 30% of the votes as required by §29 Abs. 2 WpÜG for control of a target company. Board members of HD Co. AG also contributed to the capital increase. In addition to the fact that both parties injected the company with new capital, this also sent a signal: the management, as well as the key HD Co. AG shareholder, were convinced that the company's restructuring concept would work.

The consortium's loan agreement comprised a total volume of close to EUR 80 million divided into several tranches, and it replaced the majority of the HD Co. AG's loan relationships that had been backed by individual contracts. As a consequence, the number of financing banks was reduced from more than 40 to 13 and the company had access to structured bank financing with uniform, risk-adequate provisions and extended terms. Initially, this translated into considerably less time and money spent on coordination inside of, and with, the bank circle. From the bank's perspective, the syndicated loan agreement was beneficial also, as it improved their overall collateral positions, which had originally shown many deviations. Their positions were now better aligned and more homogenous. By committing the HD Co. to additional information requirements, banks had also secured a warranty that they would receive ongoing reports on the HD Co. Group restructuring implementation status in a timely fashion.

The third financing component, mezzanine capital, was provided in the form of a subordinate credit facility in two tranches with a total value of approximately EUR 34 million. A portion of the amount was allocated to the final settlement with certain creditors who had not joined the loan consortium. The remaining amount was available for general business purposes, as well as company acquisitions. A comprehensive inter-creditor agreement dealt with the details in terms of the handling of the mezzanine facility relative to the consortium loan. The two-tranche structure also made it possible to not draw the entire loan amount in a lump sum. A portion of the mezzanine capital could thus be accessed for acquisitions when it was actually needed. Ultimately, the mezzanine facility put the HD Co. Group in a position to complete several important acquisitions during the very first year of restructuring, which further strengthened its competitive standing in the output management sector, while also providing additional flexibility thanks to enhanced liquidity in this complex restructuring scenario.

4 Experiences with the Transferability and Applicability of the Recapitalization Approach

The successful recapitalization of the HD Co. Group was made possible by four key factors:

1. A sustainable restructuring concept with a detailed business plan

2. A stable shareholder structure

3. A group of important banks who were willing to accompany the restructuring process by way of a consortium loan; and finally

4. The availability of mezzanine capital during the restructuring process

Everything hinged on the sustainability of the restructuring concept, considering that one principle applies to every reorganization: financing of a restructuring company is feasible only if the capability to be restructured and the restructuring worthiness of the company can be adequately verified. To this end, the restructuring concept must meet exacting demands: it must profile the company in its market environment, it must reveal the root causes of losses, it must encompass a concrete plan for strategic reorientation of the business, its operational and financial restructuring, as well as project the effects of the planned measures. All of this must be consolidated in a detailed business plan. The restructuring concept of the HD Co. Group fulfilled these requirements and thus provided the central premise for successful recapitalization. The subsequently launched project organization, which drove the implementation of the restructuring measures, also ensured that the implementation timetable was adhered to, and that whenever deviations from the plan were imminent, they were detected, and corrective action was taken promptly.

To adapt the capital structure to the restructuring scenario, and to strengthen the equity capital base of the HD Co. Group, an injection of fresh money in the form of equity capital was absolutely crucial. Under such conditions it is, however, quite typical that the opportunities to solicit equity capital are limited, given that no dividends can be disbursed, and the risk in terms of equity capital share value development is extremely high. In this situation, HD Co. AG could rely on its stable group of shareholders, consisting of its Asian strategic partner and its executive management, who considered their commitment to be a strategic investment, and sent a clear signal by expressing their commitment to make a major contribution to the capital increase.

The consortium banks as a group, and each individual credit institution, supported the success of the recapitalization by securing a large portion of the long-term financing of the HD Co. Group throughout the reorganization phase, thus meeting the prerequisites for HD Co. AG to obtain mezzanine capital. In conjunction with the consortium loan, some of the banks gave up justified individual interests or subjectively favorable positions in relation to collateral. Other credit institutions, on the other hand, revised fundamental decisions that had already been made, or business policy based resolutions that had aimed at the medium-term cessation of the loan commitment. At the same time, they all reaped the profits of the successful recapitalization, given that the HD Co. Group attained improved liquidity thanks to the equity capital and mezzanine financing. Moreover, the banks were able to secure improved collateral positioning for their commitments thanks to the organized provision of additional collateral in conjunction with the consortium agreement. Banks were furthermore able to push through risk-adequate pricing coherent with a restructuring scenario. Last, but not least, the banks could completely reorganize the highly fragmented creditor structure thanks to the consortium agreement and the related settlement with credit institutions who did not join the consortium.

In this case, the availability of mezzanine capital closed a critical gap through a two-pronged approach. By providing subordinated capital, the mezzanine providers not only made it possible to pay off the loan commitments of almost 30 smaller banks; they also allowed a market leader in the midst of a restructuring process to meet the requirements that would allow it to continue to grow by acquiring businesses in an industry going through a consolidation phase. After all, the realization of growth has proven to be a central factor in successfully overcoming a crisis.

Return to Growth – The Wind AG Restructuring and Recapitalization Process

Uwe Johnen, Jürgen Schäfer

1 Introduction

This case study describes the restructuring and recapitalization process implemented by Wind AG, a corporation listed on the stock exchange. This manufacturer of wind energy equipment plunged into a crisis that threatened its very existence in 2003, after its IPO and a time of turbulent growth. The root causes: operational and structural problems resulting in an unfavorable cost position and high warranty expenses, along with an abrupt downturn of the German market.

The description of Wind AG's background will provide a rough overview of the business model and the market. In the following chapters, we will describe the course that led Wind AG into a crisis. In the following section the core elements of the restructuring concept and its effects will be introduced in detail. Another chapter is dedicated to an evaluation of the financial problems Wind AG faced after its restructuring process and the resulting recapitalization concept. In closing, we will look at the lessons learned and their potential application to other businesses.

2 The Situation at the Beginning of the Restructuring Process

In 2000, Wind AG produced annual revenues of approximately EUR 400 million and claimed a global market share of around 7%. It was one of the leading suppliers of wind energy equipment. Half of the company's sales was produced in Germany. Most of Wind AG's competitors are global companies. The product portfolio focuses on high-power installations – primarily in the megawatt segment, which is the fastest growing in the industry. In addition to its core business, i.e. production and distribution of wind energy equipment, the enterprise also offers after-sales services. Wind AG is also active in project development and management. This encompasses the acquisition and management of wind park facilities, as well as the operation and sale of wind parks.

2.1 Market Situation: Strong Decline in the Domestic Market, Significant International Growth

In the future of worldwide energy supply, renewable energies play an increasingly important role. Along with biomass, wind energy is one of the fastest growing renewable sources of energy. This is particularly true for the OECD countries offering market-incentive programs. By the end of 2004, the total capacity of wind energy equipment installed globally had increased to 48,000 megawatts (MW).

From 1998 to 2003, the worldwide market grew at an average rate of about 26%. Until 2002, this progression was driven primarily by the German market, which made up around 40% of the world market from 1999 to 2002. Germany is the world's leading consumer of wind energy. Energy feed statutes and tax incentives linked to financing such equipment had created a fertile environment for this development since the 90s. Years of experience and technical innovation considerably increased the share of wind energy in the total power market.

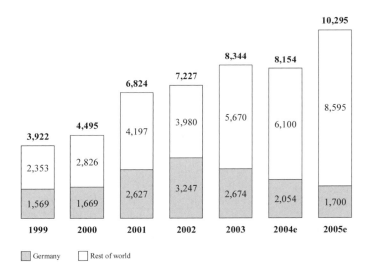

Fig. 1: Development of the German/global wind energy market [New installations, MW/p.a.]

Since 2002, however, the number of newly installed MW/p.a. has begun to drop in Germany, given that attractive sites are now hard to find and the feed compensation for new projects has been significantly reduced, limiting the amount of financing capital available. Moreover, public resistance and protests from conventional energy supply providers against the favoritism extended toward wind energy are on the rise. On the other hand, the international market continued to grow after 2002 (see Fig. 1). The trend clearly favors multi-MW facilities and, in the long term, offshore projects. Experts predict an average global growth rate of more than 14% p.a. by 2009. In the period between 2009 and 2014 growth is expected to hover around 10% p.a. These figures confirm that the wind energy market is one of the few remaining growth markets in the world.

The attractiveness of the market is also evident in the continuing consolidation of market players. In recent years multi-nationals have begun to take over the market through acquisitions, thus setting into motion a definitive concentration at the provider end.

2.2   Corporate History of Wind AG

The origins of Wind AG are in Denmark. A Danish wind equipment manufacturer founded the company in 1985, before the demand for wind energy equipment began to increase on the international scene in the first half of the 90s. From the onset, the company focused on large powerful equipment. Just two years after it had been established, the enterprise erected the then largest series installation in the world. A German corporation acquired a majority stake in the emerging company in the mid-90s and prepared an IPO. At the time, revenues and earnings were on a par with market conditions, producing growth rates of more than 20%. In 2000, the wind activities were incorporated into the new Wind AG, which began trading on the Neue Markt, a division of the Frankfurt stock exchange, on April 2, 2001. Even in the first year after going public, the success story of Wind AG continued: attaining a record revenues gain of 26% and an EBIT increase of 28%, the business was doing extremely well. Nonetheless, in the following fiscal year, incoming orders and revenues began a downward spiral driven by saturation of the German market.

Having expected a continued expansion of its business activities, Wind AG's corporate organization was dominated by a failure to concentrate resources and high structural expenditures. The speed of its organizational growth had significantly weakened process management. Moreover, Wind AG's constant striving for technical performance leadership had resulted in premature program expansions (size classes and technology) and thus translated into poorly conceived products. The consequences of taking such technical risks were evident in massive warranty expenses for equipment damage. The operational losses and the necessary accruals for warranties and restructuring translated into a loss of two thirds of the company's revenues in 2003, which virtually consumed all of its equity capital. The fulfillment of long-term delivery contracts for key components had dramatically aggravated the liquidity situation, stretching the credit lines extended by banks to the max.

3 Overview of the Restructuring Concept

As the crisis became apparent in the spring of 2003, Roland Berger Strategy Consultants was asked to support the company in developing a restructuring concept. To ensure liquidity until the restructuring process had been implemented, the banks and guarantee providers formed a collateral pool. A rough concept had to be drafted in just two months to ensure the lines would actually be prolonged. This basic concept was expanded, detailed, and implemented in the months that followed. The process comprised a total of about 2,100 individual measures. In the summer of 2004 Roland Berger also supported the recapitalization efforts of Wind AG.

3.1 The Five Core Elements of Operational Restructuring

After the initial situation had been evaluated, the restructuring concept, comprising five core elements, was introduced (see Fig. 2):

1. *Focus on attractive core markets:* although the saturation of the German market had been recognized too late and international business only made up 40% of revenues, Wind AG had been expanding worldwide in the last few years prior to restructuring. However, this expansion had not been based on a clear focus and strategy. The emphasis of this portion of the restructuring process therefore had to be concentration of the company's international positioning on the interesting core markets. A detailed analysis that included an assessment of Wind AG's competitive standing and of individual market growth pinpointed the attractive international markets Wind AG was to pursue. Markets where the company was not well positioned and that offered little potential, such as the United States, Spain, and Australia, were taken off the sales target roster. Instead, Wind AG began to focus entirely on its core markets.

2. *Regaining a technical leadership position in the upper performance segment:* the company's top priority had to be overcoming its technical weaknesses and regaining lost customer acceptance. To achieve this, the highly complex and confusing product portfolio was streamlined. The subsequent concentration on a core product portfolio focused the sales team and translated into clear positioning in the market. This process involved verifying each product in terms of its future sustainability based on earnings attained and the strategic orientation of the installations. As a result of this analysis, product complexities were reduced significantly and obsolete products were eliminated from the portfolio. The entire product line now focused on multi-MW equipment. These products were then optimized in terms of production costs, reliability and standardization, enabling the company to regain its competitive edge.

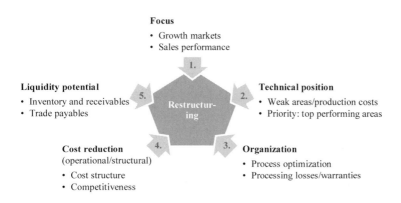

Focus
- Growth markets
- Sales performance

Liquidity potential
- Inventory and receivables
- Trade payables

Technical position
- Weak areas/production costs
- Priority: top performing areas

Cost reduction
(operational/structural)
- Cost structure
- Competitiveness

Organization
- Process optimization
- Processing losses/warranties

Fig. 2: Five core elements of restructuring

3. *Eliminating organizational weaknesses:* The rapid growth of the organization, which had gone hand in hand with the anticipated continuation of the expansive business policies, had created a number of internal Achilles' heels. During the restructuring phases a pragmatic approach was utilized to optimize the business processes. The identified weak areas, such as inadequate order/product specifications, inadequate contract management, procurement that was not order-specific, lack of central planning, and the non-existence of integrated quality management organization clearly called for improvements. The results of the process optimization measures launched was the introduction of a tender management program, and of central planning in support of sales, as well as the definition and implementation of a target process for proposal creation. The role of project management was strengthened and the introduction of integrated quality management was completed.

4. *Radical cost cuts thanks to operational and structural measures:* another central objective of the restructuring concept was reestablishing a competitive cost structure. To this end, operational and structural measures had to be defined. The structural costs were returned to a competitive level primarily by resizing the domestic sales and service operation. The closure or adaptation of foreign divisions to accommodate the strategic core markets yielded additional cost savings. At the operational end, the traditional levers of reduced staff costs and cuts in other operational expenses were obviously applied. However, cuts of about EUR 15 million p.a. could also be made in material costs as a result of new negotiations and re-negotiations.

5. *Release of liquidity potential from working capital:* due to the aggravated liquidity scenario, timely implementation of measures to uncover existing liquidity potentials was especially crucial. The three primary approaches to working capital management optimization were reduction of inventories and receivables, as well as the adequate extension of liabilities for products and

services. As a result, the level of inventory in the following fiscal year dropped by almost 50%, thanks primarily to the consumption of A components. The average term of receivables was cut to about 80 days, among other things due to the fact that more focus was placed on avoiding technical problems in the equipment shipped to customers. Supplier terms, on the other hand, were extended by ten days thanks to an increase of the target term.

In a joint effort with Roland Berger Strategy Consultants, this program was pushed through and simultaneously further developed within an implementation phase of about 18 months. In this process the planned results improvement measures aimed at about 20% of the total performance had to be significantly expanded due to the sales slump.

3.2   The Five Cornerstones of Recapitalization

After the operational restructuring phase had already progressed substantially, the final core element of the concept called for soliciting a strategic investor to address the problem of inadequate financial flexibility. This venture did fail, however, due to the high level of misgivings in relation to warranty precautions. In the going concern, the new project business secured by Wind AG also demanded additional liquidity and higher guarantee lines due to the company's negative credit ratings. The consistently restrictive liquidity policies of banks hampered the company's growth and prevented its return to the profit zone.

Consequently with the assistance of Roland Berger, a recapitalization concept was developed based on the principle that all stakeholders were to make a substantial contribution to Wind AG's restructuring process:

- Institutions who wanted to withdraw had to waive at least part of their entitlements.

- The remaining institutions were to receive results-based compensation and extend their lines.

- Existing shareholders were to accept dilutions.

- New investors were to receive a qualified majority and participate in the value growth in concert with their return expectations.

Given that one of the majority shareholders could not be considered as an investor due to its strategic orientation, a search for other financial investors began with the assistance of an investment consultant and Roland Berger's network. Numerous negotiations with the financing banks on their potential future commitment and support in the event of the entry of a financial investor took place simultaneously.

The deciding factor for successful implementation of the intended recapitalization was the ability to convince investors and banks of the enterprise's positive long-term perspective and to mediate between the various interests of all stakeholders. The sometimes diverging expectations and goals of the stakeholders had to be taken into account as the recapitalization concept was developed, so that a solution that was as close to consensus as possible could be presented. In this process it was key to not only focus on the company's super-ordinate goals to attain stable financing and realize growth perspectives, but also to take into account the interests of investors (including minimum returns, majority share in the company and exit perspectives), existing shareholders (prevention of a total loss, or participation in possible upside potential), and of the banks. Particularly the position of the banks was extremely diverse. On one hand, banks ready to exit had to be offered short-term exit perspectives, on the other hand, banks wanting to remain on-board had to be convinced that a perspective for long-term receivables value preservation did indeed exist, and that the company would be able to pay off its loans in the future.

Capital cut	Capital increase	Buyout of individual banks	Debt equity swap	Line extensions
1.	2.	3.	4.	5.
10:1	Approx. EUR **42 m** from shareholders and investors	**Three banks** bought out through haircut	Approx. EUR **28 m**, ratio 2.33:1	Additional EUR **20 m** **cash** line, EUR **40 m** **guarantee** line

Fig. 3: The five cornerstones of recapitalization

The attained compromise, which was acceptable for all stakeholders, included the following cornerstones: (see Fig. 3):

- *Reduction of the company's capital:* through consolidation of shares via simplified capital reduction, the company's equity capital of approximately EUR 50 million was reduced at a ratio of 10:1 to around EUR 5 million.

- *Capital increase:* the lowered equity capital was increased by approximately EUR 42 million via cash deposits at an issue value of EUR 1.00 per share, granting shareholders purchase rights.

- *Buy-out of individual banks:* exit-ready banks were bought out within the scope of recapitalization.

- *Debt equity swap:* conversion of cash loan receivables held by loan-providing banks in the amount of approx. EUR 28 million into equity capital valued at EUR 12 million maximum.

- *Line extensions:* extension of existing lines from loan-providing banks (additional cash lines totaling EUR 20 million and additional guarantee lines in the amount of EUR 30 million).

This concept provided a compromise that was acceptable to all parties. A clear reduction in capital, which translated into an adaptation of the nominal value to the actual value development of the company, was performed prior to execution of the capital increase. This allowed investors to acquire majority stakes in the company with a manageable investment volume.

The increase in the equity capital in conjunction with the capital increase reinforced the equity capital base and, along with the extended credit lines, gave the company the required financial flexibility. Two points in the concepts addressed the contrary positions of the loan-providing banks. On one hand, exit-ready banks were afforded a quick exit via buy-outs in conjunction with partial reductions of their receivables, while banks willing to continue their commitment were able to acquire equity capital via a debt equity swap, allowing them to participate in the business's possible long-term upside potential.

After the shareholder meeting had approved the concept the only remaining issue was how investors would be able to attain majority stakes. The shareholder purchase right allowed shareholders to maintain their existing stakes in the company in conjunction with the capital increase. Investors were thus able to acquire only those shares for which shareholders had agreed to waive their purchase rights. An exclusion of the purchase right is permissible, especially if the capital increase via cash deposits does not exceed 10% of the equity capital and the issue amount is not significantly below the stock market price (§ 203 Article 1, Sentence 1 in combination with § 186 Article 3, Sentence 4 AktG, German Stock Market Statutes). The regulation aims at providing executive management – with the approval of the supervisory board – to exclude the purchase right in order to ensure flexibility on the capital market. Given that these prerequisites were not fulfilled in this case, and consequently the purchase right could not be excluded, a high percentage of shareholders had to voluntarily give up this right to provide investors with the opportunity to acquire majority stakes, and thus put the entire recapitalization approach on a firm footing. This was achieved, ultimately, through an open letter from the board appealing to existing shareholders: they were asked to waive their purchase rights in order to safeguard the future of the company. The investors' majority stake was also not revised by the subsequent debt equity swamp by the banks, although this was performed under exclusion of the purchase right. After all, in the event of a real capital increase, the board does have the authority to exclude the statutory purchase right with the approval of the supervisory board.

In summary, the described recapitalization concept did indeed remove the financial growth hurdles Wind AG was facing while taking into account the interests of all stakeholders. The capital increase yielded a liquidity injection of about EUR 42 million, and extension of credit lines expanded the company's financial flexibility.

As a result, the balance sheet structure was significantly improved and the danger of overextension averted: the equity capital influx of approximately EUR 70 million – EUR 42 million from the cash capital increase and EUR 28 million from the real capital increase – boosted the equity capital ratio, which had been extremely low prior to the capital increase, from 1.3% to around 32%.

Wind AG proved in the very first quarter after recapitalization that the tense financial situation after a successful operational restructuring process had indeed hampered the company's development. Wind AG booked the highest volume of quarterly incoming orders in its 20-year history. Consequently, the company exceeded its own incoming order forecast, attained the planned revenue goals, and for the first time since it had been restructured, began to operate in the vicinity of the profit zone.

4 Transferable Experiences for Application of the Recapitalization Approach

Based on the experiences derived from this case study, four general success factors have been established for the recapitalization approach:

1. *Integral restructuring:* the Wind AG case study clearly shows that integral reorganization can not only be limited to cost and revenue items of the P&L, it can also include the asset side of the balance sheet as well. Approaches such as operational and structural cost cuts, as well as reduced working capital can only be a part of a comprehensive concept. The liabilities side of any corporate balance sheet must also be critically verified and possibly be realigned in the course of the restructuring process. A lack of financial flexibility, or paralyzing interest burdens, can jeopardize the future of an operationally restructured company, despite adjustment of the business to the changed overall conditions.

2. *Individual solution:* there is no such thing as a patent remedy for recapitalization; it always requires thorough concept work – particularly in the case of corporations that are traded on the stock market, where numerous restrictions must be taken into consideration. The correct individual combination of these levers improves the potential of a successful standalone strategy, as well as of the realization of strategic cooperation.

3. *Joint success:* in the long term, all stakeholders reap the benefits of a successful financial restructuring process. The company receives the required flexibility to realize its desired growth, or attains relief from an interest burden that hampers the entrepreneurial action radius. Ideally, this translates into direct benefits for the shareholders thanks to attained profits and, if ap-

156

plicable, a rising price per share. Banks enjoy a long-term perspective of loan pay off and loss avoidance. Such win-win scenarios do however hinge on accommodating the differing interests of all stakeholders, i.e. meeting their respective expectations to the greatest extent possible. Therefore, an individual solution that satisfies all interest groups must be found (see Fig. 4).

Company

Stable financial basis, securing revenues, liquidity, strategic flexibility

Banks

Sustained receivables value, rating improvement, payoff potential

Customers

Perceive company as a solid business and valuable strategic partner

Credit sale insurers

Prevention of hazards, rating improvement, declining utilization of credit limits

Suppliers

Market stabilization, safeguarding of supplier relationships, improved payment patterns

Investors

Attractive investment with long-term growth opportunities based on solid financing

Fig. 4: Financial reorganization can deliver win-win scenarios for all stakeholders

4. *Neutral moderator:* a solution that satisfies all stakeholders can only be achieved through numerous discussions and negotiations. The planned concept must be further developed and adapted to the developments continuously. To ensure this, a neutral moderator who provides ideas, develops the concept, and drives the efficient implementation of the concept, is indispensable.

The Utilization of Divestments in KML's Group Restructuring Process

1 Introduction

Injecting fresh financial resources is usually the key prerequisite in the course of corporate crises and the key condition for fighting the root causes of these crises, as well as for revitalizing the company. In Germany, most crisis companies receive their financing from loan-providing banks. In this context, stricter loan approval regulations and higher interest rates on loans have to be expected in the future. Crisis companies in particular, will have to investigate new financing alternatives. To this end, they have the option to utilize additional external financing sources.[1] However, internal financing potential will have to be used to a larger extent.

This article introduces divestment of parts of the company as a potential measure to safeguard the survival of the company and overcome the crises that jeopardize the very existence of a corporation. Divestment has already proven itself as an effective tool to secure the long-term success of businesses. Divestment has gained a more prominent role in pertinent literature, as well as practical applications, and is increasingly considered a task of strategic management.[2] Based on this concept, this article discusses a case study involving specific utilization of divestments to secure the continuation of a company in a corporate crisis threatening its very existence.

Subsequently, the cornerstones of a general model for selecting divestment objects in crises are outlined, a systematic overview of the findings is provided to assist executive management in selecting units as potential divestment objects.

---

[1]   More and more references to this type of financing can be found in industry publications. Ref. Böckenförde (1996), page 185; Buth/Hermanns/Janus (1998), page 231; Hess/Fechner/ Freund/Körner (1998), page 338f.; Kraft (2001), page 15ff.

[2]   Kötzle (1993) can be considered pioneering work in regards to a proactive divestment concept for the prevention of strategic endangerment. The publications of Thissen (2000), Rechsteiner (1995) and Weiher (1996) also take a proactive look at divestment.

The case study, as well as the model introduced, are excerpts of a completed research project of the author that is currently being published.

2 Corporate Profile and Development Before the Crisis

In the 90s, KML Group already produced revenues totaling approx. EUR 45 million in plastics and furniture function technology. In plastics, the company operated two injection-molding sites to make and distribute technical components and modules of all kinds. The activities also included in-house tool manufacturing. Key accounts for these plastic products were domestic appliance and office technology manufacturers, as well as electrical components and mobile communications suppliers, and the automotive industry.

In the furniture function segment, KML focused on the development, production, and sale of light elements utilized in furniture. Among the main products were decorative lighting, tiny integrated lighting, and flat lighting for furniture, as well as accessories such as transformers. Key clients were well-known companies in the German and international furniture industry and their suppliers.

Since the beginning of the early 90s the group had continually expanded its activities. In 1990 a first acquisition took place in the furniture function segment. The acquired company developed, manufactured, and sold furniture hardware and accessories. Among its products were decorative knobs for furniture, functional columns, and railing systems, as well as high-end furniture function systems. Just two years later, a plastics company producing medical grips and central locks was acquired.

In 1994, new and expanded facilities were erected at two production sites to meet expected capacity requirements. At the time, KML Group's revenues totaled about EUR 70 million. During that same year, two additional companies were acquired as part of the group's continued expansion, which were to form the core of the subsequent newly established merchandise presentation and lighting technology division. The acquired businesses were system providers of displays, merchandise presentation systems, and store building concepts, including ceilings and lighting for target customers in the brand products industry. The portfolio included consulting, planning, and customer-specific development services, as well as production, assembly, and financing of the products. Thanks to these acquisitions, KML Group was able to increase its sales to about EUR 110 million, achieving ordinary business results of approximately EUR 12 million.

International activities were expanded from 1995 to 1997. KML Group established additional international companies in both plastics and the furniture function technology. Moreover, KML established new production facilities, initially at its two Eastern European sites in Slovakia and the Czech Republic. In a leased facility in Slovakia, KML made technical components and plastic modules for a local branch of a well-known German client. Moreover, the new unit became a supplier for German operations of the group. The Czech facility focused primarily on job processing for the group's German companies. In 1997, a joint venture was established in Thailand, which was co-managed with a local partner. These activities targeted the company's entry into the Southeast Asian market. The new company was active in the development, production, and sale of merchandise presentation systems.

The expansion strategy continued into the late 90s. Establishing an additional merchandise and lighting technology company resulted in an expansion of existing activities. The new enterprise focused on the development, planning, and manufacture of light ceilings, and on sales and installation of these products, which included the purchase and sale of all required raw materials and support materials. The new segment targeted banks, insurance companies, hotels, government offices, and kitchen studios as new clients.

Given that total sales had increased to about EUR 125 million by 2000, a logistics center and production buildings were expanded and newly erected. The New Media business unit that developed innovative plastic CD packaging and CD business card products was established simultaneously. At the time this business was expected to produce strong growth. In 1999 and 2000 about EUR 10 million were invested in the development of this segment.

By that time, KML Group had experienced ten years of consistent expansion of its business activities and now operated four business divisions covering ten business segments, which were allocated to eleven legally autonomous companies employing 1,150 workers. Fig. 1 provides an overview of the business divisions and segments of the group.

Despite its fast-paced development, by the end of 2000, the group found itself in a crisis that threatened its survival. The following describes the root causes and how the company managed to overcome this crisis.

Business divisions	Operational companies			Business segments		
Plastics Technology (revenues approx. EUR 40 m)	Plastics 1	Plastics 2	Plastics 3	Plastic products (revenues approx. EUR 35 m)		
	Plastics 4			Belt systems (revenues approx. EUR 5 m)	Medical grips (revenues approx. EUR 0.1 m)	Central locks (revenues approx. EUR 0.1 m)
Furniture Function Technology (revenues approx. EUR 56 m)	Furniture 1	Furniture 3		Furniture hardware/accessories (revenues approx. EUR 23 m)		
	Furniture 2			Lighting for furniture (revenues approx. EUR 27 m)	Lighting & project (revenues approx. EUR 2 m	Components for vacuum cleaners (revenues approx. EUR 4 m)
Merchandise Presentation and Lighting Technology (revenues approx. EUR 32 m)	Merch. Pres. & Light.Te-chnology 1	Merch. Pres. & Light.Te-chnology 2	Merch. Pres. & Light.Te-chnology 3	Shopfitting (revenues approx. EUR 17 m)		
				Display (revenues approx. EUR 15 m)		
New Media (revenues approx. EUR 2 m)	New Media 1			CD packaging (revenues approx. EUR 2 m)		
				CD business cards (revenues approx. EUR 0.1 m)		

☐ New business areas

Fig. 1: Business division, company, and business area structure of KML Group, status 2000

3 The Crisis and the Reorganization Concept

At the end of fiscal year 2000 KML Group had maneuvered itself into a crisis that threatened its very existence. The projected loss from ordinary business operations totaled about EUR 4 million, after the group had seen continually declining results since 1994. It was also impossible to attain a positive annual result due to extensive inventory and fixed asset depreciations.

The group produced a loss of approx. EUR 11 million, which was to increase to about EUR 20 million due to planned reorganization concept measures. As a consequence, equity capital was reduced by almost half, which resulted in a drop of the equity capital ratio to 18%. The liquidity situation was ominous also, so that some disbursements had to be deferred at the end of 2000. The group was financed by banks at the rate of about EUR 65 million in debts.

The key financial indicators of KML Group are presented in Table 1.

	Actual 1998	Actual 1999	Forecast 2000
Revenues	123	124	130
Results from ordinary business operations	1.4	1.4	-4.3
Net profit	0.5	0.9	11.3
Free cashflow	-0.2	-2.2	-8.1
Equity capital	42	41	20
Number of employees (average)	1,189	1,183	1,241

Table 1: Business figures of KML Group: Actual 1998 – forecast 2000 [EUR m]

Several factors were responsible for the situation that threatened the company. One of the key causes was the extensive investment activity in new business segments, markets, and products. Investments were made; in particular in the new New Media unit, as well as international activities and product innovation, with no appropriate returns in view. In 1999 and 2000, the sum total of investments exceeded operational cash flow by about EUR 25 million.

Weaknesses in the operational business were also in evidence. The relation of gross profit per employee compared to human resource expenditures per employee had been on the decline since 1997. Moreover, inventories were increased at a rate that had an intensive impact on liquidity while extending inventory days. Ultimately, the core business stagnated while competition and price pressure intensified. The continuous expansion of the holding structure proved to be a cost burden as well. Finally, the synergy and integration potential between the individual companies were inadequate.

In the last quarter of 2000, given the situation, executive management, in concert with the funding banks, decided to develop an extensive reorganization concept with the assistance of an external consultant. The goal of the concept was to attain an ROCE of 10.5% by the end of 2002, which required significant earnings improvement totaling about EUR 13 million. To achieve this, operational and structural measures were adopted. The majority of the results improvement, i.e. about EUR 12 million, was to be attained through operational measures in the area of staff cost reductions, material expenditure savings, and miscellaneous operational expenditure cuts. Moreover, the operational measures called for improved liquidity through inventory and receivables reductions, sale and lease back as well as the sale of machines, yielding a total of about EUR 5 million.

This article focuses on structural measures aimed at realigning the business segment portfolio and its concentration on promising areas. Moreover, planned divestments and the shutdown of business divisions were planned not only to generate liquidity or minimize future loss potential, but were also supposed to reduce capital tie-up and debt. In this context, an assessment of the strategic positioning and profitability of the business divisions was performed that will subsequently be described in more detail.

The intent was to completely withdraw from the plastics technology sector through the structural measures. To this end, the divestment of the three companies Plastics 2, 3, and 4, and a portion of Plastics 1, which handled injection molding of chargers for mobile phones (hereinafter referred to as the Mobile subdivision; for information on the terms used by the companies, please also refer to Fig. 1) had been planned. Only Plastics 1 was to continue as part of the group in almost complete form.

Plans also called for cessation of the Asian activities in the merchandise presentation & lighting technology segment (Merchandise Presentation & Lighting Technology 3), while a sale of the company was to be attempted first. The shutdown of a smaller domestic trading company in this segment (Merchandise Presentation & Lighting Technology 2) was planned as well. In furniture function technology, the closure of the smaller business division Lighting & Furniture of Company Furniture 3 was targeted also; however, a divestment was considered as well.

Overall, a total of five of the eleven existing companies were selected for divestment or closure. Six to nine months were planned for this process, with the exception of Plastics 2 and 3, where the divestment was not to be completed until mid-2002. As the implementation progressed, however, some changes in relation to the structural measures were necessary that will be explained later in connection with the selection analysis of divestment objects and forms.

In summary, the structural measures led to a sustainable results improvement of only about EUR 1 million, however, a liquidity influx of approx. EUR 3 million and a reduction of capital tie-up by EUR 21 million were anticipated as well. To this end, the banks agreed to leave the liquidity attained through the divestment of the Plastics 4 company, and the Mobile sub-division were to remain at the disposal of the group and not be used to pay off of loans.

The banks were unwilling to provide additional liquidity for funding the reorganization. Only a government guarantee from the state and a shareholder contribution were available. The remaining liquidity gap had to be generated by the group through operational and structural measures.

4   The Divestment Object Selection Process

Several internal and external parties were involved in compiling and implementing the KML Group divestment program. The quality and quantity assessments of strategic relevance and value were performed, for the most part, by an external consultant and staff members from the holding company's finance department. The final selection of objects and execution of the transactions were handled by corporate management. External attorneys were integrated into the process to address legal issues. At the divestment object end, the appropriate executive management was made aware of the planned divestments, and the executive management of the holding was frequently also in charge of the companies to be divested. Employees and workers' council were only informed once the divestment actually took place.

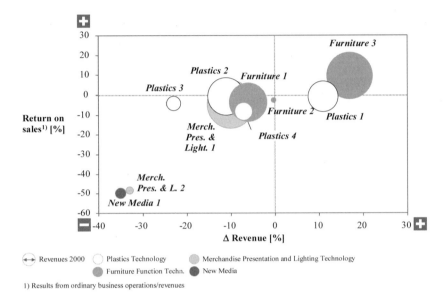

Fig. 2: Profitability segments of KML Group based on companies, status 2000

In conjunction with the structural measures, the individual business segments were analyzed based on various aspects. In this context, they were categorized as performers or non-performers. In this process the return on sales (based on results from ordinary business activities for 2000) were compared to the respective forecast, as shown in Fig. 2. A total of ten out of eleven companies were analyzed. The activities of the Merchandise Presentation & Lighting Technology 3 companies in Asia were analyzed separately.

Based on this initial analysis, the only company producing a positive return on sales was Furniture 3, making it the sole performer. Further analyses did however reveal that this did not apply to the Mobile sub-division of Plastics 1. It had advanced to a non-performing position only due to high fixed costs, which would not be incurred by a potential investor. The results of Plastics 4 were also adversely affected by goodwill write-downs and an expiring lease agreement, which would no longer impact the unit's results in the future. Given this background, these companies were considered performers as well. All other companies produced negative returns, showed increased deviations from revenue forecasts, and were thus classified as non-performers. The Merchandise Presentation & Lighting Technology 1 company attained the highest absolute negative result at a rate of approx. EUR 1.6 million, followed by the New Media division with a loss of about EUR 1 million.

The fact that almost all companies delivered negative business scenarios posed a particular challenge for executive management. Not only did management have to decide whether individual non-performers were to be reorganized, shut down, or divested; it also had to re-structure divisions and business segments of the group to develop a new, future-oriented division concept.

Based on these findings, initial rough plans for possible structural measures were reviewed; these were then verified in further analyses. One of the approaches was to sell the Furniture 3 company as the most profitable unit and to use the income to fund reorganization of the remaining divisions. Another solution option was divestment of the most capital-intensive segment, plastics technology, combined with continuation of the furniture function technology and merchandise presentation & lighting technology.

Several aspects were taken into account concerning the sales potential. In terms of in-house, stake-specific factors, positive assessments were made especially in terms of data quality. Thanks to the legal autonomy of the enterprises and an efficient EDP system, it was extremely high with all of the companies.

In terms of overall company-specific criteria, special emphasis was placed on economies of scope. Interdependencies between Plastics 1 and Furniture 3 were found. The in-house revenue percentage of Plastics 1 with Furniture 3 totaled about 50%. Moreover, both companies shipped their products to the same customers. Selling both of these units would have been feasible as a package only. This did not apply to Plastics 1's Mobile sub-division. Similar relationships were also detected between Plastics 2 and 3, which were closely linked operationally. The same was true for Furniture 1 and 2. The remaining units did not offer any major economies of scope.

In terms of external factors, the individual divisions and companies differed. Plastics technology was considered highly attractive in this context. Two or three competitors were considered to be prospective buyers, given that they would have been able to attain synergies through an acquisition. This assessment was based on production costs as well as target customers. To this end, competitors would have been able to improve their position with key accounts and would have become their largest suppliers. Performer Furniture 3 was considered to be similarly attractive, since it would have been attractive to potential competitors thanks to its positive results. Given their minimal business activities, the Merchandise Presentation & Lighting Technology 2 and 3 companies received low grades in terms of attractiveness for potential investors.

In selecting the divestment objects, the stakeholders also played a relevant role. Looking at the customer base of Plastics 2 and 3, companies that already showed a high level of operational linkage, it was determined that they primarily served the same customer roster. Executive management presumed that the isolated sale of one of the two businesses would adversely affect the customer relations of the other company. This supported the assessment that only a joint sale of both companies would be feasible. Customer links could also be found between Furniture 1 and 3.

The banks and the majority shareholder also influenced the selection process. The majority shareholder considered the young segment New Media particularly promising. Some of the loan-providing banks supported reorganization and continuation of the Merchandise Presentation & Lighting Technology company. It was the only company with autonomous financing; the corporation funded all of the other divisions centrally.

In making the ultimate selection decision, the very detailed assessment of strategic relevance of the divisions played a central role. The assessment of the individual business segments was based on their market attractiveness, competitive strength, and profitability. Profitability was assessed based on ROCE. In terms of market attractiveness and competitive strength, a scoring model was developed. The respective criteria and weighting are shown in Fig. 3.

	Market attractiveness		Competitive strength	
Criteria/ weighting	1. Market development	40%	5. Relative market share	40%
	2. Price development	20%	6. Services offered	15%
	3. Market return	20%	7. Success factors	45%
	4. Market conditions	20%	– Price	
			– Quality	
			– Know-how	
			– Punctuality	
			– Innovation	
			– Service/consulting	

Fig. 3: Scoring model for market and competitive assessment

In this context, the market and competitive analyses were based on management's assessment of the business segments, which was complemented by external customer survey results. The respective findings for the business segments are shown in Fig. 4. The New Media business division was initially excluded because the opportunities and risks would be evaluated in conjunction with a marketing concept that was still being compiled.

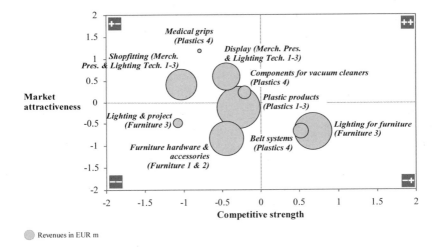

Fig. 4: Results of the market analysis and competitive analysis of KML Group based on business segments

In terms of the performers that were needed to fund the group reorganization, it was determined that the furniture lighting business segment, which consisted of the Furniture 3 company, held the strongest competitive position, and that it was considered to be the primary core business, and was thus to be sold as a last priority. The two other performers, Plastics 4, and the Mobile sub-division, on the other hand, were found to be less relevant in terms of strategy. Moreover, their activities were not part of KML Group's core business.

Non-performers, just like performers, were evaluated for strategic relevance based on market attractiveness, competitive strength, and importance for the core business. Initially, it was decided to shut down the Light & Project division of the Furniture 3 company, given that it focused on a smaller non-core activity with high negative returns, minor strategic relevance, and low sales potential. Based on its small size it was also assumed that the costs of shutting it down would be covered by the income from asset sales. The same was true for the group's Asian activities, the Merchandise Presentation & Lighting Technology 3 company, and for the smaller Merchandise Presentation & Lighting Technology 2 company, whose expansion to critical size would have required substantial financial resources. However, prior to shutting down both of these companies, a search for a potential buyer was to be conducted.

The decision as to which of the large non-performers in the three major business divisions should be sold off or closed down, and which areas would be reorganized proved to be far more difficult. To this end, the Merchandise Presentation & Lighting Technology division with its store building and display segments was found to enjoy higher market attractiveness than business segments plastics products, furniture hardware & accessories.

In order to make a decision, the feasibility of reorganization was analyzed for each of the respective companies. The goal for the units was to produce an ROCE of 10.5% after the reorganization. It was determined that this goal did not appear to be attainable for companies Plastics 2 and Furniture 1, while Furniture 1 was more relevant for the core business and the company held a leading position in its market. The high capital intensity also raised another red flag in terms of continuation of Plastics 2. Moreover, large investments had just been made in a Furniture 1 plant. For the remaining non-performers, reorganization was deemed a realistic route to take.

The divestment program, which was subsequently adopted, comprised performers Plastics 4 and the Mobile sub-division. In coordination with the banks it was agreed that income from the sale would remain at the disposal of the group to fund its reorganization and would not be used to pay off loans. In relation to non-performers, it was decided to divest Plastics 2 given its negative strategic position and the assumption that it could not be reorganized, although it had good sales potential. Moreover, the indebtedness of the group could be significantly reduced, given that assets of the unit were utilized as collateral for loans. Given the close association with Plastics 3, the latter was allocated for divestment as well. This translated into an almost complete withdrawal from the plastics sector. Plastics 1 however, was to remain with KML Group due to its linkage with the furniture function technology and positive assessment of its reorganization potential. Table 2 provides an overview of the planned measures.

The effects of the planned divestments, shutdowns, or closures were included in business plans for the individual divisions and consolidated into an overall plan, which comprised P&L, balance sheet, and liquidity planning.

In terms of performers and non-performers allocated for divestment, an assessment based on the discounted cash flow method (DCF) was performed. The presumed planning scenarios comprised the operational reorganization measures that increased the value of the respective division. Association effects were not to be considered, given that the sole entities with operational links, Plastics 2 and 3, were to be sold as a package. Synergies attained by potential buyers were not taken into account in the planning process. Purchase price discounts were also not calculated. To calculate the result or liquidity effects, the book values or liabilities to be adjusted in conjunction with the divestment were taken into account. The effects entered into the plan simultaneously provided the lowest possible purchase price threshold.

Business division	Company	Classification	Sales potential	Strategic relevance	Divest-ment	Reorg./ continua-tion	Closure
Plastics Technology	Plastics 1	Non-performer except one sub-division	High	High	(X Mobile)	X	
	Plastics 2	Non-performer	High	Low	X		
	Plastics 3	Non-performer	High	Low	X		
	Plastics 4	Performer (after adjustment one-time effects)	High	Low	X		
Furniture Function Technology	Furniture 1	Non-performer	Average	Average		X	
	Furniture 2	Non-performer	Average	Average		X	
	Furniture 3	Performer (except business division Lighting & Project)	High (low for div. Lighting & Project)	High		X	(X Lighting & Project)
Merchandise Presentation & Lighting Technology	Merch Pres. & Lighting T. 1	Non-performer	Average	Average		X	
	Merch. Pres. & Lighting 2	Non-performer	Low	Low			X
	Merch. Pres. & Lighting 3	Non-performer	Low	Low			X
New Media	New Media 1	Non-performer	-	-	-	-	-

Table 2: Analysis results and divestment program KML Group
(Source: In-house presentation based on data supplied by KML Group)

For the non-performers to be reorganized, the respective sub-plans including reorganization measures, were entered into the overall plans of KML Group. If a shutdown was planned, the shutdown plan for the respective units was incorporated in the overall planning. This was also true for units that were to be shut down, for which divestment attempts were still to be made, given that a sale was considered highly improbable.

As the reorganization concept was implemented, some changes did come up that required a completely new concept of structural measures, and thus of the divestment program. The high level of flexibility and executive management's ability to react quickly were the sole saving graces that prevented a failure of the reorganization.

While, in terms of performers, Plastics 4 could be divested as planned, the Mobile sub-division encountered significant changes. The key client, a supplier for a large mobile radio provider, had decided to procure its products from China and failed to extend the existing contractual relationships. This resulted in the total collapse of the Mobile sub-division's business, which simultaneously rendered the unit worthless for any potential investors. The only option remaining was to sell individual machines owned by the sub-division and to close down operations. The planned liquidity effects that were crucial to the reorganization thus could not be realized.

The next major setback occurred with the non-performers. The units allocated for shutdown were handled as planned with no impact on the results and liquidity of the company. A buyer was also found for the Merchandise Presentation & Lighting Technology company in Thailand, who was willing to pay at least a minimal purchase price. However, the divestments of plastics divisions 2 and 3, and the reorganization of divisions Furniture 1 and Merchandise Presentation & Lighting Technology 1 were fraught with problems.

Both of the plastics companies developed better than planned. The reorganization measures that had been initiated in conjunction with the divestment activities could be implemented quickly, allowing the units to attain positive developments in terms of results and liquidity. Nevertheless, no buyer could be found who would have paid the planned purchase price scheduled to lower the group's debt. The events surrounding divisions Furniture 1 and Merchandise Presentation & Lighting Technology 1 deviated from the planned development as well. The markets continued their downward spiral for both companies, so that the planned reorganization measures were not sufficient to achieve a recovery. Both divisions continued to call for short-term unplanned liquidity support.

KML Group's executive management reacted immediately to these developments. New analyses were quickly completed. They indicated that the market and competitive situation would improve in plastics function technology, while the prospects in the business segments, Furniture 1 and Merchandise Presentation & Lighting Technology 1 would see a downturn.

A decision to keep plastics companies 2 and 3 and to withdraw from the two other units was made accordingly. A strategic buyer from the industry could be found for Furniture 1 at short notice. The buyer acquired the company for EUR 1 and no further liquidity had to be made available for the division. In concert with the financing banks, insolvency proceedings were initiated for Merchandise Presentation & Lighting Technology 1. It appeared to be the only possible alternative given that the foreseeable obligations could not be financed, and it was impossible to find a buyer quickly. Due to the fact that the unit had obtained independent financing and had never been integrated into the group operationally, no negative consequences for the group or potential liabilities had to be taken into account.

As a final alteration to the original concept, the New Media division was not continued, given that analyses performed in the interim promised only minor potential for short-term profits as a result of these activities. The unit was thus shut down, and all machines could be sold to a manufacturer of blank CDs. Despite high machine depreciation costs, the income from sales did cover the shutdown costs, allowing the group to generate a large percentage of the missing liquidity caused by the failed divestment of the Mobile sub-division.

Overall, despite the ultimate changes that had to be made to the structural measures, the survival of KML Group could be ensured and the sustained profitability of the companies active in the remaining segments (plastics technology and furniture function technology) could be ensured by 2003 as planned.

5 Findings and Approaches for a General Model

In analyzing the key divestment success factors in the case of KML Group, several factors surfaced. First, the selection of the subsidiaries was of crucial importance. It was vital to select divisions that could be divested in the market quickly and easily thanks to high sales potential. In this context, the importance of the market environment for divestments was once again underlined. Moreover, experience showed that non-performers were less problematic to divest if the divestment was concluded at a purchase price of EUR 1 and a positive continuation option for the unit could be shown. Moreover, speed and purchase price could be increased when the division could be divested to investors with an industry connection who were able to realize potential synergies through the acquisition. It proved easier to find buyers for the divestment of units with a positive business development than for non-performers. As a final issue, the need for great flexibility and fast reaction in the event of unexpected changes in the implementation of measures in general, and divestment measures in particular, was addressed.

From these experiences, key findings can be gleaned that, as stated in the introduction, allow development of a general model based on a completed evaluation. This article discusses only the basic approach and the structure of the model in brief. In this context, divestment is viewed from two perspectives in connection with crisis situations. On one hand, the divestment of corporate divisions does provide an opportunity to generate financial resources; on the other hand it provides an option for alternative approaches to reducing the need for financial resources. The former aspect focuses on the question of which subsidiaries have to be sold to attain the greatest possible influx of financial resources without significantly weakening the company as a whole. The latter aspect analyzes the extent to which divestment provides a suitable alternative in comparison to reorganizing a division that currently shows a negative financial development, for example.

Principally, the developed model allows the analysis and reconciliation of the financial resource potential attainable by divesting performers, and of the liquidity and equity capital needs required to solve the problems of non-performers. The structure of the model is based on the sequence of the analyses that will be performed and consists of four modules. In this context, the sequence does not have determining characteristics, so that some of the analyses can also be performed simultaneously. The basic structure is shown in Fig. 5.

The first module covers the classification of the business segments and divides the subsidiaries into performers and non-performers, thus allowing initial prioritization for subsequent analyses. The goal is to identify subsidiaries that consume the greatest amount of liquidity and equity capital and those subsidiaries or business segments that produce the most.

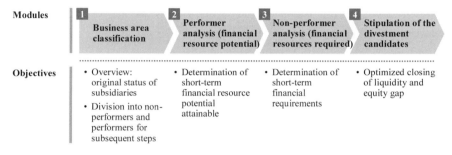

Fig. 5: Modules and objectives of the selection model in crises

The second module aims to determine short-term liquidity or equity capital to be potentially produced by divesting performers. This analysis therefore focuses solely on the divestment options. A filtering process is utilized to determine the subsidiaries that can be sold at short notice. It first addresses the sales potential, and then the sustainable value of the subsidiary. The goal of the filtering process is to determine those subsidiaries that can be sold at short notice and their liquidity and equity capital generation potential. In an additional step, to arrive at a final ranking in the divestment sequence, the strategic importance of the subsidiary is considered in addition to the financial and economic criteria. It is therefore ensured that subsidiaries that are of minor strategic relevance are sold first in order to close the liquidity and equity capital gap. Subsequently, this module determines the financial resource potential that can be unleashed by divesting subsidiaries that can be sold at short notice and whose sale does not significantly damage the strategic positioning of the remaining corporate entity.

Module three then reviews the non-performers. The objective of the analyses performed is to provide medium to long-term optimum alternatives that solve the problems of non-performers and to derive the financial resources required to implement them. The point of departure is the assessment of short-term sales potential, and the strategic relevance of the subsidiary. Contrary to the performer analysis, this approach does not directly determine any divestment candidates. The optimum medium and long-term alternative is derived from these analyses. Divestment provides an additional option to continuation and reorganization, as well as shutdown of the respective subsidiary. Upon determination of the alternatives for the respective subsidiary, business plans are compiled to calculate the financial resource requirements for non-performers. The author would like to emphasize that a final selection of an option is not yet made at this point.

The fourth module allows consolidation of the findings attained in the second and third module, and determination of the divestment candidates. To this end, the financial resources required are compared with existing potential. First it is analyzed to what extent the financial resources needed for the alternative handling of non-performers can be covered by divesting performers without strategic relevance. If coverage is insufficient in terms of liquidity or equity capital, then additional performers can be divested or alternatives for the non-performers can be selected that spare the financial resources.

In the detailed layout of the model, the individual tools and analytical methods required for the individual modules are described in detail, thus allowing the generation of an objective and analytically feasible divestment program tailored to the crisis situation of the company. This provides corporate managers with a tool for the target-oriented utilization of divestments in situations that threaten a company's survival.

Bibliography

Böckenförde, B. (1996): Unternehmenssanierung (Corporate Reorganization), 2nd printing, Stuttgart.

Buth, A. K./Hermanns, M./Janus, R. (1998): Finanzwirtschaftliche Aspekte der Fortführung von Krisenunternehmen (Financial and Economic Aspects of the Continuation of Companies in Crisis). In: Buth, A. K./Hermanns, M. (Editors): Restrukturierung, Sanierung und Insolvenz (Restructuring, Reorganization and Insolvency). Munich, pages 224-245.

Buth, A. K./ Hermanns, M. (1998): Grundsätzliches und formelle Aspekte zur Beurteilung von Sanierungskonzepten (Principal and Formal Aspects in the Assessment of Reorganization Concepts). In: Buth, A. K./ Hermanns, M. (Editors): Restrukturierung, Sanierung und Insolvenz (Restructuring, Reorganization and Insolvency). Munich, pages 351-361.

Hess, H./Fechner, D./Freund, K./Körner, F. (1998): Sanierungshandbuch (Reorganization Manual). 3rd printing, Neuwied et al.

Kötzle, A. (1993): Die Identifikation strategisch gefährdeter Geschäftseinheiten (The Identification of Strategically Endangered Business Divisions). Berlin.

Kraft, V. (2001): Private Equity Investitionen in Restrukturierungen und Turnarounds (Private Equity Investments in Restructuring and Turnarounds). Frankfurt/Main.

Rechsteiner, U. (1995): Desinvestition zur Unternehmenswertsteigerung (Divestment for Increased Corporate Value). Aachen.

Thissen, S. (2000): Strategisches Desinvestitionsmanagement: Entwicklung eines Instrumentariums zur Bewertung ausgewählter Desinvestitionsformen (Strategic Divestment Management: Development of a Tool for the Assessment of Selected Forms of Divestment). Frankfurt/Main et al.

Weiher, G. (1996): Das situative Desinvestitionsmodell. Entwicklung eines Instrumentariums zur Entflechtung diversifizierter Unternehmen (The Situative Divestment Model. Development of Tools for the Decartelization of Diversified Companies). St. Gallen.

About the Authors

Blatz, Michael, has a degree in engineering. Michael Blatz has been providing consulting services to Roland Berger Strategy Consultants clients since 1990, focusing on restructuring and strategic reorientation. Michael Blatz became a Partner in 1998 and has been head of the Restructuring & Corporate Finance Competence Center for two years.

Address:
Roland Berger Strategy Consultants, Alt-Moabit 101b, 10559 Berlin
michael_blatz@de.rolandberger.com

Brunke, Bernd, is a Partner at the Restructuring & Corporate Finance Competence Center of Roland Berger Strategy Consultants in Berlin. He provides consulting services to business executives all over Europe and in the United States. His client roster comprises medium-sized companies and multinationals and his focus is on business restructuring. Bernd Brunke came onboard in 1996 and was made a Partner in 2001.

Address:
Roland Berger Strategy Consultants, Alt-Moabit 101b, 10559 Berlin
bernd_brunke@de.rolandberger.com

Falckenberg, Max, studied business administration at Passau University, Berlin's Humboldt-University, and the Haas School of Business at the University of California, Berkeley/USA. He has been a Certified Public Accountant (CPA) since 1999. Prior to joining Roland Berger Strategy Consultants in 2000, he worked for KPMG in Berlin, London and Düsseldorf for five years. Max Falckenberg has been a Principal at the Restructuring & Corporate Finance Competence Center since 2004, where he focuses on trade and construction.

Address:
Roland Berger Strategy Consultants, Karl-Arnold-Platz 1, 40474 Düsseldorf
max_falckenberg@de.rolandberger.com

Foerschle, Stephan, studied law and business administration in Heidelberg, St. Gallen (Switzerland), at the London School of Economics and at Columbia Business School in New York. During his studies, he gained professional experience at Proctor & Gamble and in investment banking at Deutsche Bank. In 2002, he joined Roland Berger Strategy Consultants' Restructuring and Corporate Finance Competence Center as a Consultant. His work focuses mainly on operational restructuring and strategic reorientation in the media business, manufacturing industries and private equity.

Address:
Roland Berger Strategy Consultants, Alt Moabit 101b, 10559 Berlin
stephan_foerschle@de.rolandberger.com

Haghani, Sascha, Dr. rer. pol.: After industry training at a pharmaceutical company, he studied economics in Freiburg im Breisgau, and later business administration in Switzerland. He initially joined the Restructuring & Corporate Finance Competence Center at Roland Berger Strategy Consultants in 1992 as a freelancer and became a consultant in 1994. In January 2000 he was elected Partner. His focus is on financial restructuring of medium-sized companies and strategic reorientation, especially in the retail, wholesale and construction industry.

Address:
Roland Berger Strategy Consultants, Karl-Arnold-Platz 1, 40474 Düsseldorf
sascha_haghani@de.rolandberger.com

Huber, Florian, has worked for various law firms and as a trainee at Hypovereinsbank. He joined Roland Berger in 2001 after having completed his second state examination in law and passing the bar exam in Munich. Florian Huber is an Expert in Roland Berger's Business Intelligence unit, where he is in charge of product development. He has extensive experience as an author for a number of publications, and as content advisor for Roland Berger's Challenge Club.

Address:
Roland Berger Strategy Consultants, Arabellastraße 33, 81925 Munich
florian_huber@de.rolandberger.com

Johnen, Uwe, studied business administration and engineering in Aachen. He has been a member of the Restructuring & Corporate Finance Competence Center team since 1996, after first acquiring five years of consulting experience. As a Partner at Roland Berger Strategy Consultants, Uwe Johnen heads restructuring and strategic reorientation projects, with a focus on engineering and automotive suppliers.

Address:
Roland Berger Strategy Consultants, Alt-Moabit 101b, 10559 Berlin
uwe_johnen@de.rolandberger.com

Kraus, Karl-J., studied business administration, focusing on corporate management, strategy and marketing. After first paying his professional dues in the industry (among others, he worked for the Fichtel & Sachs Group for five years) he began his career as a consultant with Roland Berger Strategy Consultants in 1981. In 1984, Karl-J. Kraus advanced to Associate Partner; in 1986 he became a full Partner of the company. In 1990 he began to develop the Berlin office as well as the Restructuring & Corporate Finance Competence Center. From 1994 to 1999, Karl-J. Kraus was a member of the Management Committee. From late 1999 to June 2003 he was the chairman of the Management Committee Germany. In addition to his operational engagement, Karl-J. Kraus was elected vice chairman of the Roland Berger Beteiligungs GmbH supervisory board on July 1, 2003. Moreover, he is the advisory board chairman of CMP Capital Management Partners GmbH and holds several other supervisory board mandates.

Address:
Roland Berger Strategy Consultants, Alt-Moabit 101b, 10559 Berlin
Karl-J_Kraus@de.rolandberger.com

Kuhlwein von Rathenow, Nils R.: After completing his studies of business administration, he worked in industry and for a large financial auditing firm before he joined Roland Berger Strategy Consultants in 1997. In the summer of 2002 he was appointed Partner of the Restructuring & Corporate Finance Competence Center of the company.

Address:
Roland Berger Strategy Consultants, Karl-Arnold-Platz 1, 40474 Düsseldorf
nils_von_kuhlwein@de.rolandberger.com

Kuhnt, Ivo-Kai: After industry training with a leading international electronics conglomerate, he studied business administration in Bayreuth. In 2002 he joined Roland Berger Strategy Consultants as a consultant for the Restructuring & Corporate Finance Competence Center. Ivo-Kai Kuhnt's key clients are chemical and oil companies.

Address:
Roland Berger Strategy Consultants, Karl-Arnold-Platz 1, 40474 Düsseldorf
ivo-kai_kuhnt@de.rolandberger.com

Lafrenz, Karsten, Dr. rer. pol., studied business administration at the Westfälische Wilhelms-University in Münster and corporate finance at the University of Strathclyde in Great Britain. He holds a degree in Business Administration and a Master of Science in Finance. Following his studies, he joined the Restructuring & Corporate Finance Competence Center of Roland Berger Strategy Consultants as a consultant in 2000 and has been of Project Manager since 2004. In 2003 he received his doctorate from the European University Viadrina in Frankfurt/Oder for his thesis on value-oriented reorganization management.

Address:
Roland Berger Strategy Consultants, Alt-Moabit 101b, 10559 Berlin
karsten_lafrenz@de.rolandberger.com

Moldenhauer, Ralf, Dr. Ing., studied economic engineering (technical specialization machine engineering) at the Technical University at Darmstadt. He began his career as a consultant in 1994, joining the Roland Berger Strategy Consultants team at the Restructuring & Corporate Finance Competence Center. Since January 2000 he has been a Partner in the company. While working, he completed his dissertation on the subject of "Crisis Management in the New Economy" and received his doctorate from the Berlin Technical University in 2003.

Address:
Roland Berger Strategy Consultants, Alt-Moabit 101b, 10559 Berlin
ralf_moldenhauer@de.rolandberger.com

Paul, Christian, studied economics in the United States and obtained his MBA from Oxford University. He then worked for a large financial auditing firm for two years and was recruited by Roland Berger Strategy Consultants in 2000. He has been a Project Manager since 2004. Christian Paul focuses on financial restructuring of medium-sized companies.

Address:
Roland Berger Strategy Consultants, Alt-Moabit 101b, 10559 Berlin
christian_paul@de.rolandberger.com

Piehler, Maik, Dipl.-Kfm., studied business administration at the Leipzig Graduate School of Management and at the A.B. Freeman Business School (Tulane University) in New Orleans. He began his career with Roland Berger Strategy Consultants at the Restructuring & Corporate Finance Competence Center in 2002, specializing in portfolio and liquidity control and the recapitalization of medium-sized companies.

Address:
Roland Berger Strategy Consultants, Alt-Moabit 101b, 10559 Berlin
maik_piehler@de.rolandberger.com

zu Putlitz, Julian, Dr. rer. pol., studied political economics at universities in Bonn, Munich and Zurich. After working three years as a scientific assistant at the Friedrich-Schiller-University in Jena he received his International Management doctorate from the Otto-Friedrich-University in Bamberg. His career as a consultant began in 1998, when he joined the Restructuring & Corporate Finance Competence Center at Roland Berger Strategy Consultants. Since 2004 he has been a Partner. His consulting work to date comprises the restructuring and recapitalization of medium-sized companies, the restructuring of insolvent companies, as well as the design and implementation of restructuring programs for large corporations.

Address:
Roland Berger Strategy Consultants, Alt-Moabit 101 b, 10559 Berlin
julian_putlitz@de.rolandberger.com

Richthammer, Michael, studied business administration at Regensburg University and at the Leipzig Graduate School of Management (HHL). After completing his studies, he was recruited by Roland Berger Strategy Consultants for the Restructuring & Corporate Finance Competence Center in 2004.

Address:
Roland Berger Strategy Consultants, Karl-Arnold-Platz 1, 40474 Düsseldorf
michael_richthammer@de.rolandberger.com

Schäfer, Jürgen, completed industry training at a machine and equipment manufacturer. He then studied business administration at Cologne University. He has been a member of the Restructuring & Corporate Finance Competence Center consultant team at Roland Berger Strategy Consultants since 2004.

Address:
Roland Berger Strategy Consultants, Alt-Moabit 101b, 10559 Berlin
juergen_schaefer@de.rolandberger.com

Sievers, Gerd, Dr. rer. pol., studied business administration in Cologne and has been a Restructuring & Corporate Finance Competence Center consultant with Roland Berger Strategy Consultants since 1994. In 2004 he received his doctorate from Rostock University for his Ph.D. on the subject of "Divesting Corporate Investments in Crisis Situations".

Address:
Roland Berger Strategy Consultants, Alt-Moabit 101b, 10559 Berlin
gerd_sievers@de.rolandberger.com

Simon, Robert, Dr. rer. pol., studied business administration with a focus on corporate accounting, taxes, organization, and information technology at the RWTH Aachen and received his doctorate for his thesis on material flow control in the automotive industry. Subsequently, he worked in logistics and sales for BASF AG for several years. He has also been Managing Director of the Saarbrücker Zeitungsgruppe and the DGM-Deutsche Gesellschaft für Mittelstandsberatung. Dr. Robert Simon is a Restructuring & Corporate Finance Competence Center Partner at Roland Berger Strategy Consultants.

Address:
Roland Berger Strategy Consultants, Alt-Moabit 101b, 10559 Berlin
robert_simon@de.rolandberger.com

Waldow, Björn: After industry training in banking, he studied business administration at Mannheim University and the London School of Economics and Political Science. In May 2002 he joined the Restructuring & Corporate Finance Competence Center at Roland Berger Strategy Consultants in Berlin. As a Senior Consultant he focuses on the financial restructuring of corporations.

Address:
Roland Berger Strategy Consultants, Alt-Moabit 101b, 10559 Berlin
bjoern_waldow@de.rolandberger.com